Past-into-Present Series

INVENTIONS

Graeme Kent

B. T. BATSFORD LTD London

First published 1971
© Graeme Kent, 1971

Filmset by Keyspools Ltd, Golborne, Lancs.

Printed in Great Britain by Billing & Sons, Guildford, Surrey
for the Publishers
B. T. BATSFORD Ltd, 4 Fitzhardinge Street, London W1
7134 1768 4

Contents

Acknowledgment

The Author and the Publishers wish to thank the following for the illustrations appearing in this book: Aerofilms Ltd for fig. 5; Australian News and Information Bureau for fig. 1; Barnaby's Picture Library for fig. 39; Bodleian Library for fig. 8; British Aircraft Corporation for fig. 60; British Hovercraft Corporation Ltd for fig. 59; British Railways for fig. 51; Daimler-Benz Museum, Stuttgart for fig. 29; Daily Mirror Newspapers Ltd for fig. 50; Digital Equipment Co. Ltd for fig. 58; Ford Motor Company Ltd for fig. 40; Hawker Siddeley Aviation Ltd for fig. 62; Imperial War Museum for figs. 48, 49, 53, 54, 55, 56; Keystone Press Agency Ltd for fig. 61; Linotype and Machinery Ltd for fig. 23; Trustees of the London Museum for fig. 37; Mansell Collection for figs. 4, 7, 10, 11, 12, 15, 21, 22, 27, 32, 33, 34; Museum of Rural Life, University of Reading for fig. 31; National Film Archive for figs. 42, 43; National Maritime Museum for fig. 20; National Portrait Gallery for fig. 13; Popperfoto Ltd for fig. 2; Radio Times Hulton Picture Library for figs. 9, 14, 16, 18, 24, 25, 26, 28, 30, 38, 41, 44, 46, 52; Royal Postgraduate Medical School for fig. 57; Science Museum for figs. 3, 6, 17, 19, 45; Tracked Hovercraft Ltd for fig. 63; Trustees of the Wellcome Institute for figs. 35 and 36.

The Illustrations

1 Out of the Darkness

The First Inventors

Men did not make tools at once. It took many thousands of years for them to develop this ability. Only slowly did they make the change from naked, homeless wanderers to people able to look after themselves and live in some degree of comfort.

We do not know when men first made tools. It must have happened at different times in various parts of the world. It seems possible, however, that about 40,000 years ago men had discovered that stones, especially flints, could be sharpened and used as cutting and scraping tools. These crude pieces of rock were the first inventions of mankind.

We give the name of the Old Stone Age to this period when people were starting to fashion such tools and weapons. Other developments followed. After the first scrapers and cutters men went on to make axes and wooden spears with stone heads. Their descendants went further and invented other tools, fish-hooks and even bows and arrows.

By the time of the New Stone Age, perhaps 10,000 years ago, men had made more inventions. Using their stone tools they had developed sledges on wooden runners to drag the carcasses of animals they had slain. They had also hollowed out tree trunks to make dug-out canoes in which to cross rivers without getting wet.

1 Early men developed implements of stone and flint in order to scratch a living from the soil. This modern Australian aborigine is using the same sort of sharpened stone tool that primitive men used hundreds of thousands of years ago.

The Settlers

These inventions made it possible for men to hunt more easily. They could also make simple clothes from animal skins. But they were still wanderers, almost always on the move in search of food.

Hundreds of years passed in this way. Men made other inventions which eased their lives a little. The wheel was developed. This made transport more convenient. People learned how to make fire for themselves by rubbing flints together.

Then came another great milestone in the progress of the human race. About 8,000 years ago some men began to settle down. They stopped being wanderers and hunters and became farmers.

On the banks of such rivers in the Middle East as the Nile and the Euphrates, men discovered that the climate was pleasant and the ground fertile. Crops could

2   In some parts of the world men still use ploughs not very different from the first ones to be invented. The first farmers burnt the vegetation on the ground and buried their seeds in the ash. From this they proceeded to scratching shallow trenches in the soil and planting their seeds in these holes. After a while they constructed larger digging sticks which had to be hauled over the ground by two men while a third steered. Eventually farmers used beasts of burden to drag the ploughs.

be planted and grown for food and then more seeds put into the ground. Instead of always being on the move men could stay in one place for long periods.

In order to grow and harvest the wheat and other crops, men discovered the need for more tools and similar implements. They began to experiment and then developed such aids as ploughs, hoes and flails. At first the farmers dragged their ploughs over the ground themselves; later they tamed wild animals and harnessed oxen and asses to the ploughshares.

Because men were now staying in one spot for long periods, farmers started to build primitive dwelling places for their families. Over the centuries these homes improved from holes in the ground to small huts. Men invented bricks of sun-baked mud, and 5,000 years ago many villages, especially in the Middle East, were constructed of these bricks.

Before long it became obvious that stone tools were no longer efficient enough for what was required of them. Something stronger was needed. In the ground men found metals which could be heated and mixed together and then hammered into tools. First they used copper, then bronze and finally iron.

These metals were responsible for whole new industries coming into being. Some men became miners to dig the metals from the earth. Others became smiths to melt and mix them, and then make them into ploughs and tools.

Other inventions were necessary in order to make the beasts of burden work properly. The horsemen of Asia invented the bridle and the bit for their animals. These inventions were copied by the people of Europe and the Middle East.

Three thousand years ago men were living in what we now call the Iron Age. By that time there were many different inventions and discoveries in use.

The Middle East

One of mankind's earliest civilisations was among the nations of Egypt and Mesopotamia, where men first settled as farmers. Over 3,000 years ago the Egyptians were using the wheel in order to drive machinery. They also developed the pulley to shift heavy weights, and were building ships with sails which were crossing the Mediterranean Sea on trading voyages.

The Egyptians invented one of the first forms of writing. This consisted of pictures, each with a different meaning. They also developed the writing material called papyrus and constructed an efficient calendar. Their public buildings and monuments were larger than any seen before. Thousands of men, working under Egyptian engineers, built the Great Pyramid containing five million tons of stone and standing 450 feet high. Long ditches were dug to allow water from the rivers to flow past farm land and irrigate the crops.

In Mesopotamia the Sumerians invented the type of writing known as cuneiform script, in which symbols were impressed upon clay tablets. The people of this region were also famous for their carvings and jewel work. They were among

3 Egyptians constructing a canoe out of papyrus reeds about 2,600 years ago. In these vessels the Egyptians sailed across the Mediterranean Sea, but because that area was often smooth and windless, they also had to make provision in their ships for oarsmen.

the first to make pottery on a potter's wheel, while their neighbours the Assyrians did a great deal of work in iron and the Babylonians constructed bridges and roads.

China

Another great early civilisation was to be found in China. The Chinese invented a form of printing long before it was used in Europe. The Chinese of this early period also invented explosives. They had a highly developed civilisation when parts of Europe and the whole of North America were still in the early Iron Age.

The Greeks

One of the best known of all early civilisations is that of the Greek Empire. Yet although the Greeks were highly cultured, few great inventions came from them. They developed the use of the lathe for wood turning, but as they had so many slaves to perform menial tasks, they saw little need to construct labour-saving devices.

One exception to this rule was an inventor and mathematician called Archimedes. Among his mathematical discoveries was a method of working out the number of grains of sand on a beach. But it is for his inventions that Archimedes is remembered. During his lifetime he was responsible for at least forty.

Archimedes lived in the city of Syracuse on the island of Sicily, and the King of Syracuse made sure that Archimedes used his skill for the good of the city. One invention, for which he seems to have been at least partly responsible, is called the Screw of Archimedes. This was a sort of gigantic corkscrew. It sucked up water and caused it to run uphill for short distances, and was used a great deal for draining marshy areas.

Archimedes was interested in levers and their use in moving heavy objects. He once joked that if he could make a lever long enough he would be able to move the world.

Towards the end of his life Syracuse was besieged from the sea by Roman ships, and Archimedes turned his talents to inventing machines which would drive the Romans away. At first he was successful; he designed great grappling hooks, worked by a system of levers and pulleys. These hooks were lowered on to the Roman ships from the walls of Syracuse. They lifted the vessels from the sea and dashed them against the rocks on the shore.

But even the genius of Archimedes could not keep the Romans away for ever. In 212 B.C. they stormed the city and captured it. In the fighting Archimedes was killed.

Another famous inventor who lived before the birth of Christ was Hero of Alexandria. We know little of his private life, but he experimented with such things as gear wheels, pulleys, a fire engine and mechanical toys.

4 The aelophile, a primitive steam turbine, of Hero of Alexandria. Hero left several treatises from which it is clear that he was aware of a number of mechanical devices, including arrangements for using the force of steam.

11

5 Roman roads were either laid over old tracks or constructed straight across the country, like this one near Chichester in Sussex. London was the centre of the road system. The Roman soldiers each carried a saw and a pickaxe and were as accustomed to building roads as they were to fighting.

The Romans

For a time the Romans were the most powerful people in the known world. Their armies were triumphant almost everywhere and they made considerable use of machines invented by other nations; the Romans used these inventions to strengthen their armies. Such weapons as huge catapults were built. Men specialised in digging tunnels under the earth and throwing bridges across rivers in order to speed the progress of the legions of solidiers.

Above all the Romans built roads. Wherever they went their engineers laid down strong, straight highways. At the peak of the Roman Empire there were 50,000 miles of roads built by the Romans throughout their possessions.

The Dark Ages

The Romans reigned supreme for hundreds of years, but eventually even their mighty empire came to an end. It was destroyed by wild raiders from the North called Goths. The Romans withdrew their armies from England and other outposts in order to defend Rome itself.

As soon as the legions left, other raiders swept in. In England, first the Saxons and then the Vikings invaded the country and occupied it. The civilisation of the Romans was destroyed and then largely forgotten. By the beginning of the 5th century A.D. it looked as if the greater part of the known world was going back into the darkness from which it had emerged thousands of years before.

Further Reading

Quennell, *Everyday Life in Prehistoric Times* (Batsford)
Quennell, *Everyday Things in Ancient Greece* (Batsford)
Quennell, *Everyday Life in Roman and Anglo-Saxon Times* (Batsford)
Miliken, *The Roman People* (Harrap)
Kent, *Topics Through Time* (U.L.P.)
Alexander, *The Past* (Parrish)
Grimal, *Stories from Babylon and Persia* (Burke)

2   The Middle Ages

The Arabs

By the end of the 7th century A.D. the Arabs had taken the place of the Romans as the most powerful people in the world. Their armies spread out from the Middle East in all directions. They conquered Egypt, swept into Europe to occupy most of Spain, and reached the borders of India. By the year 732 A.D. the Arabs owned a large and powerful empire.

They were not inventors themselves but took up and used the inventions of the people they conquered. They also gathered together and wrote down the wisdom and learning of earlier civilisations.

Among the knowledge that the Arabs kept alive was that of the Greeks, especially the writings of a man called Aristotle. Aristotle had lived 300 years before the birth of Christ. He had studied science, nature and politics, and the results of his studies, written down and kept by the Arabs, were later used by European scientists in their work.

As early as the 1st century A.D. the Chinese had invented paper. The Arabs captured a number of Chinese paper-makers and forced them to give up the secret of the paper-making process. By the year 1100 there were a number of paper-making factories in the Middle East, and before long some were opened in Europe.

6   An astrolabe of the sort once used by the Moors in the Middle East. It could be used for navigation both on land and at sea, and it was also used by teachers of astronomy.

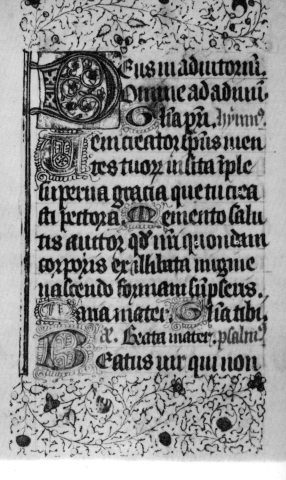

7 A page from a handwritten book of the fifteenth century. Such books, generally written in Latin, were rare and expensive, usually the prized possessions of the wealthy few. They were often ornately designed, and the letters beautifully illustrated, by monks.

Arab mathematicians and scientists were very interested in astronomy and did a great deal of work in plotting the course of the sun, but the only major invention that came from the Arabs seems to have been the lateen sail. This was a sail in the shape of a triangle which ran the entire length of a ship. It took the place of the square sail which had been used by the Romans.

Revival of Learning in Europe

Slowly the learning of the past which had been written down by the Arabs found its way to Europe. Some scholars had continued to study in the monasteries. By the 12th century such scholars as Adelard of Bath and Robert of Chester were making their way to Spain and Sicily to study the writings of the Arabs and bring back the knowledge contained in them to Europe.

Before this the monasteries had provided shelter for men who wished to think and study. The monks had also made many improvements in hand-written books. Often these books were very beautifully designed. We hear about one of these books in the 10th century. A bishop called Asser was writing about the boyhood of Alfred, later to be king of Wessex:

On a certain day, therefore, his mother was showing him and his brother a Saxon book of poetry, which she held in her hand, and said, 'Whichever of you shall the soonest learn this volume shall have it for his own.'

Alfred won the book, which he must have prized greatly as such objects were both rare and expensive.

Although we hear of few inventors working in monasteries, many of these men who had given up their lives to the service of God do seem to have been students of science. Often their work made it possible for inventors in later times to do their experimenting and manufacturing.

One such pioneer in England was Roger Bacon, a Franciscan friar. Bacon worked in Oxford in the 13th century and was known as a great teacher. He did much research into eyesight; he also dreamt of inventing ships powered by engines and machines which one day would fly through the air. Such ideas frightened people and Bacon was put into prison.

Weapons

Even in the Dark Ages, one form of invention still went on—the efforts of men to make more and more powerful weapons with which to fight one another. The man with the strongest fighting implement usually won the fight. In earlier times such articles as wooden clubs had been used, then stone axes and stone-headed spears were developed. Finally, with the discovery of metal, men began to design swords and daggers.

The smith, the man who made these weapons, was a powerful man. He often ate at the same table as his king, a great honour. We can get some idea of the variety of weapons used in this description of the arms on board a Saracen ship in 1191: '. . . one hundred camel-loads of arms, slings, bows, darts and arrows'.

In the 14th century, however, a great change was brought about when a German, whose name is unknown to us, invented gunpowder. He probably obtained the idea from the Arabs who in turn had copied the fireworks of the Chinese. Roger Bacon had also been interested in the possibility of developing something with the effect of gunpowder and had written about it.

As with most inventions, gunpowder led to the development of many other new things. As late as the 14th century bows and arrows had been the main means of fighting at a distance. Writing about the Battle of Crécy, in which the English fired their arrows at the Genoese soldiers fighting for France, a man called Froissart said:

When the Genoese felt these arrows, which pierced their arms, heads and through their armour, some of them cut the strings of their crossbows, others flung them on the ground, and all turned about and retreated quite discomfited.

The introduction of gunpowder changed warfare. No longer could men retreat to safety behind the walls of their castles. In order to use the gunpowder

8 An illustration from a fifteenth-century chronicle of the Battle of Hastings (1066). The knights on horseback are wearing body armour, and the horses have saddles and bits, inventions made soon after the horse was domesticated. The foot-soldiers have little protection. The bows and arrows in the picture were among the first weapons to be invented and other weapons here are the short sword of the knight and the lances towering above the fighting men.

to its best advantage men invented and built great cannon, first of iron and later of bronze. The balls fired from these cannon could demolish the walls of many fortresses.

In the same way the armour which men had worn to defend themselves against blows from swords and axes was no longer of much use, and was gradually discarded. None of this happened at once, of course. Old and new methods of fighting continued to be used together for some time. There is an account of a sea fight in 1512 which demonstrates this:

> The fight was very cruel, for the archers of the English part, and the cross-bows of the French part did their uttermost: but for all that the English entered the carrack, which seeing, a varlet gunner being desperate put fire in the gunpowder . . . and set the whole ship on fire.

Building

Some progress was also made in the building industry, especially in such public buildings as churches and palaces. Architects and builders introduced new ideas to make their work easier. For hundreds of years masons had copied the buildings of the Romans with their solid, imposing arches and pillars. Gradually, however, the ideas of the Arab builders began to be introduced into Europe, especially after the return of Crusaders from the Middle East. The buildings of the Arabs were taller than those of the Romans and had pointed arches instead of the curved Roman ones. European architects began to experiment with mixtures of both styles. One of the most famous architects of the Middle Ages was Erwin

17

von Steinbach, a German who built many famous churches.

Another new development in building was the introduction of theatres. At first bands of actors performed wherever they could. Then platforms were built on to the side of churches for the production of religious plays. Finally special theatres were constructed for the actors.

Gutenberg and the Invention of Printing

One of the most important inventions developed in Europe in the Middle Ages was that of printing. In fact, some authorities have said that the invention brought the Middle Ages to an end as the new supply of books brought education and enlightenment to many more people.

As we have seen, the Chinese had developed a form of printing, but the wooden blocks that they used were not strong enough to produce vast supplies of books. Books had to be copied out by hand, mainly in the monasteries.

Johannes Gutenberg changed this. Born some time between 1394 and 1398 the young German showed that he had a great aptitude for anything mechanical. He became very interested in the possibilities of inventing a printing machine. It is possible that he heard of pioneer work done by a Dutchman called Coster.

Gutenberg knew that something stronger than wood must be found for the type used in printing. Among his other talents he was a goldsmith and knew something about metals. He used this knowledge when he made his first experiments. Using brass punches in the shape of letters he made impressions in lead. These impressions, each one in the form of a different letter, he used as moulds. From these moulds Gutenberg made the letters, known as typeface, which he used in his new printing machines.

His experiments took many years but they succeeded. In 1456 he completed a printing project which convinced people of the strength and power of his new

9 *Left* Part of the bas-relief on the monument of Johannes Gutenberg, who developed the first adjustable typecasting apparatus. The bearded Gutenberg is seen comparing the finished printed sheet with the original manuscript. The workman is operating the printing press.

10 *Right* A page from a book printed in the English tongue, as it then was, by William Caxton who brought the printing press to England. The story illustrated is from Aesop's fable about the fox and the grapes.

¶ The fyrst fable maketh mencyon of the foxe and of the rapsyns

He is not wyse/ that desyreth to haue a thynge whiche he may not haue/ As reciteth this fable Of a foxe/whiche loked and beheld the rapsyns that grewe vpon an hyghe vyne/the whiche rapsyns he moche desyred for to ete them ¶ And whanne he sawe that none he myght gete/ he torned his sorowe in to Ioye/and sayd these rapsyns ben sowre/and yf I had some I wold not ete them/And therfor this fable sheweth that he is wyse / whiche fayneth not to desyre that thynge the whiche he may not haue/

¶ The second fable is of the auncyent wesel and of the rat/

Wytte is better than force or strengthe / As reherceth to vs this fable of an old wesel / the whiche myght no more take no rats/wherfor she was ofte sore hongry process. In that year Gutenberg completed printing, in Latin, a Bible over 1,000 pages in length.

As soon as Gutenberg's achievement became known, other men took it up. Printing works opened in many different countries. In England, a former merchant called William Caxton set up a printing works near Westminster Abbey to produce the first books printed in the English language. Other men were printing books in their languages. It is estimated that by 1500 over 16,000 different works had been printed in over 200 different places.

In succeeding centuries printing machines were used to produce newspapers in order to spread news and information. Printing undoubtedly was responsible for a great deal of progress.

11   This sketch from the notebooks of Leonardo da Vinci shows a proposed weapon, some form of gigantic crossbow. As well as being a magnificent artist Leonardo was a brilliant inventor and engineer and for a time advised the warlike prince Cesare Borgia on weapons.

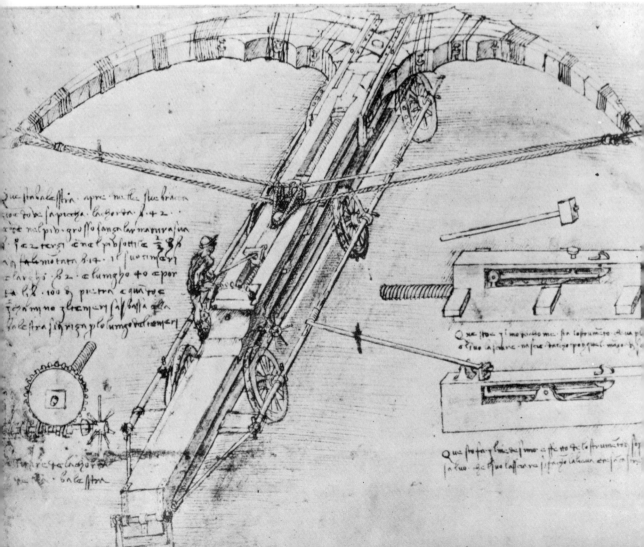

Leonardo da Vinci

One of the most versatile men who ever lived was Leonardo da Vinci. He was born in Italy in 1452. Today we remember him chiefly as a magnificent painter, but he was also an engineer, a designer and an inventor. When he was a young man, he wrote a letter to the Duke of Milan asking for work and giving a list of his qualifications:

> I have a way of making bridges that shall be strong, light and easy to move. I know how to burn or destroy the bridges of the enemy. When a place is besieged I can build ladders and covered ways. I know how to destroy a fortress, even if it is founded on rock, without using cannon. I can make portable cannons, made so that they fling a storm of stones and make much smoke. When it comes to a naval battle, I have many machines. I can build my own vessels that cannot be sunk by guns.

Leonardo spent 16 years working for the Duke of Milan. In that time he drew up the plans for a number of inventions. He designed a steamship, although he did not make an engine for it. He also spent a great deal of time in trying to design a flying machine, and studying the movement of birds and bats in flight.

After his death, Leonardo's notebooks were to be found full of plans and drawings for inventions. Few if any of them were ever constructed. Leonardo spent so much of his time in painting such portraits as the 'Mona Lisa', and working as an engineer for Italian princes like Cesare Borgia, that he never put his designs for inventions into practice.

Communications

Slowly men emerged from the Dark Ages which had possessed Europe for so many centuries. There are a number of reasons for their eventual progress. There was a great revival of learning and art called the Renaissance, which spread education and knowledge. The work of such people as Roger Bacon and Johannes Gutenberg also helped to pass on new ideas.

Another reason was the improvement of communications, that is of roads, canals, ships and other methods of travel. Different trades and industries were improving and merchants wanted to be able to take merchandise from one country to another. In order to do this men had to invent better and more convenient ways of getting about and transporting goods.

Somewhere about the year 1200 seamen seem to have invented a rudder capable of directing ships through the roughest seas. Two hundred years later the Portugese invented sailing vessels with three masts which enabled them to sail even farther. Another invention of seagoing men was a method of keeping fish fresh by packing them in salt on their journey from the fishing grounds to the markets.

By the 16th century men had realised the necessity for improving sailing methods and all other means of transport. New compasses made navigation more reliable. Other inventions were equally useful.

Other Inventions

There were a number of reasons for encouraging inventors by the 16th and 17th centuries. Different trades and industries were trying to improve their methods of production. People were eager to buy their goods if enough could be manufactured. Different nations were in competition with one another. Each country wanted to be better than its neighbours, so inventors were urged to produce fresh machines and appliances to improve industries.

In order to supply the raw materials for the various trades and industries there was an increased demand for more coal and metals. This meant that miners turned their energies to improving mining methods and thereby increasing the amount of material brought out of the earth. In England, by the reign of Elizabeth I, many houses were burning coal for fuel, which meant an even greater demand for the product of the coal mines and led to still more streamlined methods of mining.

Scientists in this period of new learning were making discoveries which were to help inventors in their work. One scientist who did a great deal towards modernising scientific thought was Galileo.

Galileo Galilei (1564–1642) was one of the first experimental scientists; this means that he tried to put his theories into practice. He constructed a powerful telescope and spent years studying the movements of the planets. He became very interested in the theories of a Polish astronomer called Copernicus. Copernicus (1473–1543) had come to the conclusion that the sun, not the earth, was the centre of the universe.

After a great deal of research Galileo said that he agreed with Copernicus. He stated his belief that the earth moved round the sun, not the sun round the earth. This caused a great deal of trouble. The Church authorities were shocked by what they thought to be a wild idea. Galileo was brought to trial before the Inquisition and forced to declare that he was wrong. Today of course we know that his theory was the correct one.

However, the work of Copernicus and Galileo encouraged other men to think for themselves. Many people tried to find out more about the world in which they lived. It could be said that the age of inventions was about to begin.

Further Reading

Unstead, *The Medieval Scene* (Black)
Baker, *The Early Middle Ages* (Hutchinson)
Salzman, *England in Tudor Times* (O.U.P)
Milward, *The 17th Century* (Allen and Unwin)
Quennell, *A History of Everyday Things in England, Vol. 1* (Batsford)
Johnson, *Tools and Machines* (Oliver and Boyd)
Escott, *Cathedrals and Churches* (Oliver and Boyd)

3   The Need for Inventions

Causes of the Industrial Revolution

There were three main reasons for Britain's great leap forward in farming and industry. In the first place merchants and other wealthy men were willing to put their money into new methods, thus encouraging growth. The second reason was the fact that there was so much coal available for mining in Great Britain. This coal provided the fuel to power new inventions. The third reason lay in the number of brilliant men who invented the machines which enabled Britain to become the leading industrial nation of the 19th century.

The Inventors

Among the early British inventors were such men as the Darbys. Thanks to their experiments, blast furnaces could be powered by coal instead of charcoal, supplies of which were growing scarce.

The textile industry was transformed by a number of British inventors. In 1733 John Kay invented the flying shuttle. The cotton industry was given an additional impetus by James Hargreave's spinning jenny, while the machine tools of men like Bramah and Maudslay helped in almost every manufacturing industry.

Men like James Watt experimented with steam power which was to drive the factory looms and later the railway locomotives and steamships. Other inventors were equally important in the growth of other industries.

Cloth Making

Cloth making, or the textile industry as it is called, has been important in Great Britain for hundreds of years. Even before the Industrial Revolution, English wool was famous for its quality.

Until various machines were invented, cloth making was a slow and costly business. In 1618 it was calculated that a clothier who made 20 broad cloths a week would need to employ about 500 people for all the processes necessary. Obviously this was not a good way of doing business. Anyone who could invent a machine to do the work of some of these 500 people would have a great effect on the cloth making trade.

The first man to come up with a revolutionary invention was John Kay with his flying shuttle, or fly shuttle, which came into regular use in 1733. This shuttle consisted of a little box on either side of a machine called a loom. It was designed

23

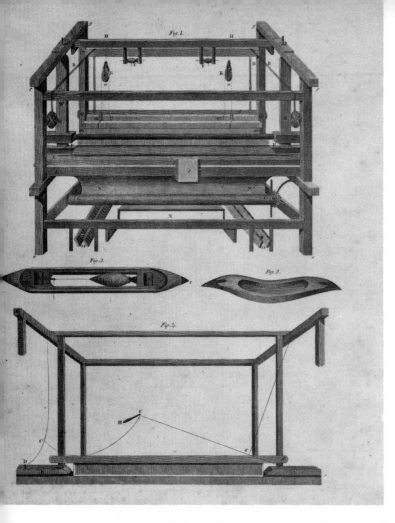

12 John Kay's flying shuttle, shown here in diagram form in a contemporary magazine, helped to speed up the various processes of weaving. On the earliest looms, a number of threads were held tautly. These threads were known as the warp. The weaver would then lace other threads (the weft) across the warp thus forming cloth. Using Kay's flying shuttle a workman could operate a wide loom unaided.

to help in the construction of cloth so that one man could do the work previously done by two.

Unfortunately this frightened the workers, who thought that by using this machine half of them would be put out of work, and they drove Kay away from the Colchester factory where he had introduced his shuttle. He moved on to several different towns with no greater success. In Leeds, factory owners used his machine but did not pay him. At Bury, his house was attacked by cloth workers who thought that he had come to take away their jobs. Kay escaped in a roll of cloth and made his way to France, where he died a deeply unhappy man.

But other inventors followed in Kay's footsteps. In 1768 James Hargreaves invented the 'Spinning Jenny', a spinning machine named after his wife. This could do the work of several men. Later machines devised by Hargreaves were able to do the work of many people. Again workers got to hear of this. They burst into the inventor's home and smashed his machine. Hargreaves managed to escape and later opened a small factory using his machines.

All the early inventors of machines to speed up the cloth making industry had to contend with the resentment of the workers who were afraid that these machines would take away their jobs. Richard Arkwright designed a machine for producing

13 Richard Arkwright, 1732–92. Arkwright's claim to fame as the inventor of the water frame and roller-spinning machine has been seriously questioned by historians. But there is no doubt that his career is one of the best examples of the way thrusting, energetic businessmen can use the inventions and discoveries of others to their own advantage.

14 Arkwright's water frame. His spinning machine included the principle of drawing rollers. These inventions revolutionised the textile industry.

a great deal of yarn cheaply. Not only did he have to flee from Nottingham and later have one of his mills burnt by workers, he also had to contend with factory owners who used his machine but tried to avoid paying for it. Arkwright was tougher or luckier than many of his fellow inventors because he died a rich man.

Less fortunate was Samuel Crompton who designed an improved 'jenny' which he had to take to pieces and hide in case factory workers heard of his experiments. Crompton was also treated badly by industrialists who used his machine without paying him. Crompton was a shy, retiring man and this treatment made him bitter. In the end he was granted £5,000 by the English Parliament, but other men made much greater fortunes from his invention.

Nevertheless, the work of Kay, Hargreaves and the others laid the foundations of Britain's textile industry. Their machines made the various processes of cloth making both cheap and easy. This in fact led to employment for many thousands of people, especially in Lancashire and other Northern areas.

Heavy Industry

Britain was to become known as the workshop of the world. Her factories, powered by English coal, fashioned steel and other heavy goods famous for their strength and quality. The mines which produced the coal, and the factories making the goods, owed much to the machines and appliances designed by British inventors.

Before the 18th century British coal mining had not been an efficient process. The Romans in Britain had used what coal they had found on the surface. After they left no coal seems to have been mined until about the year 1100 and perhaps not until as late as 1200. After that, for five or six hundred years, coal mining consisted mainly of gathering coal washed up from the sea or exposed on the shore by the action of the waves, and of 'open cast' mining, which was the digging of coal from shallow trenches near the surface. This was gradually extended until pits some way underground were constructed; but mining remained inefficient and costly for a long time.

Then a number of events made the large scale production of coal an important matter. Abraham Darby, a farmer's son, set up a small foundry and smithy. At first he used peat and charcoal to provide power, but he made experiments with coal. His son, also called Abraham, carried on with these experiments, and by 1770 this man's son-in-law was running one of Britain's largest foundries, using coal. The work of the two Darbys and of Richard Reynolds, the son-in-law, encouraged other factory owners to change over to coal. This in turn led to a demand from mine owners for engineers to invent improved mining techniques.

Such techniques began to appear. As early as 1631 David Ramsay tried to make mining safer by perfecting a device for getting rid of excess water from pits. In 1712 the Royal Society gave its approval to a steam operated pump for getting rid of water, a major hazard to miners. James Spedding developed a system of ventilating pit shafts by a system of doors and walls, while Clanny and George Stephenson both worked on miners' safety lamps which would not set fire to the gas found below ground. Such a lamp was later improved by Davy.

All these inventions were aimed at making mining more efficient. They could make the miner's life a little safer, but they could not make it much more pleasant. Mining continued to be hard work; men, women and childred toiled below ground for long hours to produce coal. They produced it in ever-increasing quantities, and this was all that mattered to most industrialists and factory owners.

In the factories themselves further improvements were made. Joseph Bramah,

15 Coal mining in 1556 was a precarious affair. Here we see miners employing a number of methods of getting down the mine shaft. One is climbing down a ladder, a second is being lowered on a winch by two fellow workers, a third seems to be sliding down while clinging to a rope, and a fourth is descending by some steps cut in the rock.

16 Small factories and workshops were in existence as early as the sixteenth century. In this illustration of 1568 a man weaving is seated at a loom while a woman is supplying him with fresh threads. Silk could be woven at a loom as well as cloth, and as the cloth trade grew so the buildings which housed the workers became larger.

the son of a Yorkshire farmer, started his career as an inventor by experimenting with the design of new locks. He then went into partnership with Henry Maudslay and in 1795 developed a hydraulic press. This was a piece of equipment used in the construction of bridges and such ships as the gigantic *Great Eastern*, which was designed by Brunel. This press was powered by water and was much more efficient than earlier methods.

After Bramah's death Henry Maudslay went on to invent more tools, including a special lathe. A lathe was a piece of machinery which kept objects moving in a circular motion. Maudslay was helped, and finally succeeded, by a Scot named James Nasmyth. Nasmyth went on to invent a number of machines to speed up factory processes. He was to compare his machines favourably with the work people in the factories:

> The machines never got drunk; their hands never shook from excess; they were never absent from work; they did not strike for wages; they were unfailing in their accuracy and regularity. . . .

Power

Many inventors were concerned with the problem of power. They were looking for more powerful ways of propelling the machines which produced goods, and

28

for methods of making transport quicker and easier by sea and land.

In 1704 Denis Papin, a Frenchman, designed an engine powered by steam. Papin had spent a great deal of time working on this problem. He had first been attracted to the subject when King Louis XIV of France asked a Dutchman named Huygens to design an engine that would provide power to pump the water of the many fountains at the palace of Versailles.

At the time Papin had been Huygens' assistant. The two of them made many experiments but did not produce a workable engine. Papin's imagination had been fired by the prospect of developing such a machine, and he went to live in England where he could work with an English scientist named Boyle.

Boyle and Papin conducted a number of experiments concerned with air and gas pressure. In the process of this work Papin invented a new type of saucepan which made its contents boil more quickly than other saucepans on the market.

Eventually Papin went to work for the Landgrave of Hesse, a German prince, and carried on with his experiments to produce an engine. At first he thought that gunpowder would be the best way of powering such an engine, but his experiments with models convinced him that steam was the answer. He invented such an engine, complete with a cylinder and pistons, which turned water into steam and had enough power to drive things along. Of this invention Papin wrote in 1705:

> I can assure you that the farther I proceed the more highly I learn to esteem this invention, which in theory must increase the powers of man to an infinite degree. As to the practical side, I think I can state without exaggeration that, with the aid of this machine, one man will perform the work of any other hundred.

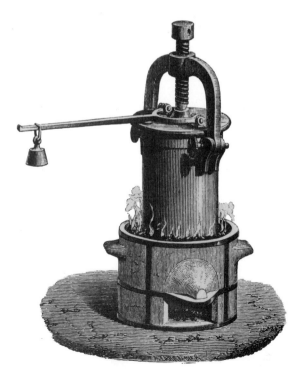

17 Denis Papin came to England in 1675 to work with Robert Boyle, the scientist. The two men conducted a number of experiments connected with air and gas pressure. They also made experiments with a pneumatic pump. Then in 1681 Papin invented the pressure cooker seen above. The lid screwed on to this cooker made the contents boil more quickly.

Most of Papin's experiments had been conducted with models. When he was satisfied that he was ready to build a real steam engine he made plans to return to Britain where he hoped to be able to raise the money for its construction. With

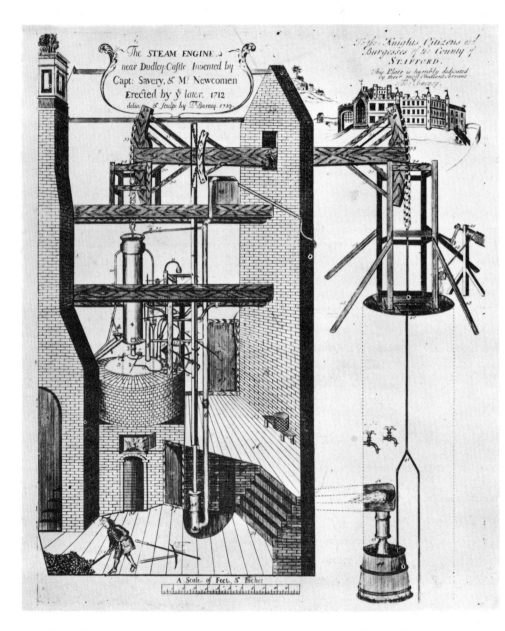

18   One of the first steam engines was a pumping engine designed by Thomas Newcomen, patented in 1705. It consisted of a large timber beam which swung on a pivot and was pulled down by a piston rod in a large cylinder. This lifted a bucket of water out of a mine shaft. The one seen in this picture was installed near Dudley Castle about 1712.

the little money he had left he purchased a paddle boat, hired a crew and set off to make the journey to Britain via the rivers of Germany.

All went well until the paddle boat reached the city of Munden. The citizens of Munden disliked vessels from other cities sailing past. They refused to allow Papin's ship to pass. Papin lost his temper and attempted to paddle past Munden. The citizens of Munden, enraged, pulled the ship ashore and destroyed it.

Eventually Papin reached Britain, but he seemed to have lost heart. For ten years he carried on with his experiments but never accumulated enough money to build a steam engine. He died a poor man in 1712.

Papin was a pioneer, he had paved the way for other inventors to experiment with steam engines. One of these men was Thomas Newcomen, a Dartmoor blacksmith, who invented a steam-driven engine for pumping water out of mines. Other inventors also worked on the problem of steam engines; the most famous of these was James Watt.

Watt was born in Greenock in Scotland in 1736. He was a sickly child but his father, a carpenter and merchant, saw to it that he went first to a grammar school and was then apprenticed to a mathematical instrument maker in London. He became friendly with a Dr. Black, a well-known chemist, and was appointed mathematical instrument maker at Glasgow University.

19 As the notice on this machine says, it is the model of the Newcomen engine at Glasgow which James Watt repaired in 1765, and in so doing, discovered ways in which it could be improved. The idea of a separate condenser, however, which would save on the amount of fuel needed in the Newcomen engine did not come to him in a flash; for several years he experimented and his engine was not patented until 1769.

One day, while he was still a young man, Watt was asked to repair a model of Newcomen's steam engine. He did so, but in the process became dissatisfied with its construction. Watt was not a fast worker but he kept pondering over the problem of improving upon Newcomen's design. Two years after he had dismantled Newcomen's engine he had an idea which he later wrote about:

> I had gone for a walk and my thoughts turning naturally to the experiments I had been engaged in for saving heat in the cylinder, the idea occurred to me that, as steam was an elastic vapour, it would expand, and rush into a previously exhausted space. . . .

This gave Watt the idea of designing a separate condenser which would save up to three-quarters of the fuel needed by Newcomen's engine. The latter provided $4\frac{1}{3}$ million foot-pounds of energy from one cwt of coal, while from one cwt Watt's engine gave 39 million foot-pounds of energy.

Watt gave up his instrument-making business to devote himself full-time to his invention. It was not easy work. The Scot ran into debt, and almost ruined his health. Finally he was helped by an industrialist, Dr. Roebuck, who paid off Watt's debts and supported him for a time, but eventually lost all his own money and had to sell his interest in Watt's engine. His place was taken by Matthew Boulton, another industrialist who owned workshops at Birmingham. With Boulton looking after the financial problems and providing constant practical help, Watt was able to press on. In 1781 he developed an appliance which powered the piston of his engine.

This device was the breakthrough that he needed. His engine could now provide power for the machines of any factory without any outside help, and the idea was taken up at once. Some people stole Watt's idea and used variations of his appliance without paying him; Watt took them to court, and much of the last ten years of his life was spent in legal actions against people who had tried to use his steam engine without paying for it.

Like many inventors Watt ended his life embittered by what he regarded as the poor treatment he had received from factory owners. But no one can deny the influence he had on his time: thanks to his development of the steam engine Britain became established as the major industrial nation of the world.

Other 18th Century Inventors

Among other innovators of the early era of the Industrial Revolution were such men as Josiah Wedgwood, John Harrison, William Murdock, John MacAdam and James Brindley.

Josiah Wedgwood, like James Watt, suffered greatly from ill health. He was born in 1730 and apprenticed as a potter to his brother Thomas. While Wedgwood was not primarily an inventor he adapted the inventions and ideas of other people to produce some of the best-known pottery in the world. He introduced efficiency and high standards into the manufacturing processes when he opened his own potteries in Staffordshire. He made sure that his craftsmen worked at only one task instead of changing from one process to another. Although increasingly in pain (at the age of 38 Wedgwood had a leg amputated) he refused to pass shoddy work, personally touring his workshops and smashing faulty work and equipment.

The cups and saucers produced by Wedgwood's factories became world famous by 1770. Not only were they well made, they were beautifully designed. Wedgwood was also a good employer: his factories were well run, adequate housing was supplied for his workers, and surrounding roads and canals were modernised to allow his wares to travel without being smashed in transit. Josiah Wedgwood died in 1795 after a long and painful illness.

While Wedgwood was primarily a man who used other men's inventions, John Harrison was an inventor in his own right. In 1761, this son of a carpenter invented a chronometer which proved to be the most accurate time-keeping device used up to that time on sea voyages. In a 6-week journey to the West Indies, Harrison's chronometer lost only five seconds.

20 This chronometer, made by John Harrison in 1759, was tested on a journey to the West Indies and was always accurate to within five seconds. In order to double check its accuracy the Admiralty insisted on a duplicate being made to Harrison's specifications by another watchmaker. The duplicate (right) was equally satisfactory.

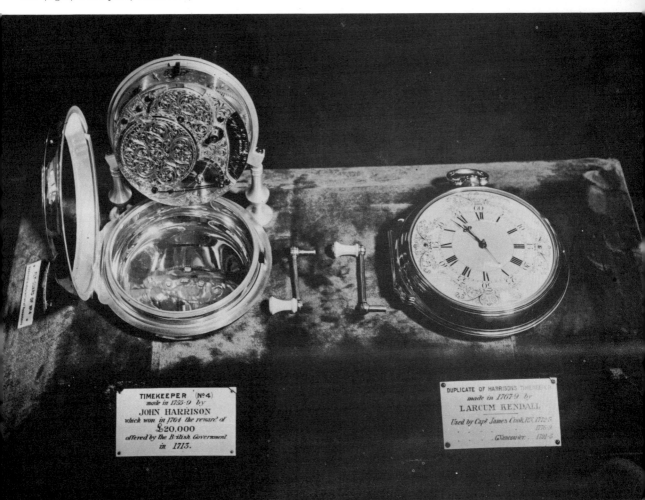

21 Many working people were highly suspicious of the new machines of the Industrial Revolution. They thought that these machines, performing more quickly the work done previously by men, would deprive them of their livelihood. Here we see John Kay, inventor of the flying shuttle, forced to flee from angry weavers.

William Murdock worked as a young man with James Watt and was sent to the mines of Cornwall to help with experiments on pumping machinery. As was the case with many engineers, Murdock attracted a great deal of hostility from the suspicious workers. Unlike most engineers, however, Murdock was a big, strong man. After several miners had attacked him and been severely beaten by the Scot, Murdock was left in peace to carry on with his experiments.

He made a number of improvements to Watt's steam engine, constructed a form of gas lighting, and even developed a small steam-driven carriage, but was prevented from carrying on with these inventions by Watt who asked Murdock to concentrate on improving the mine pumping machinery in Cornwall.

Communications were a great problem in 18th-century Britain, and two pioneers in improving travel were John MacAdam and James Brindley. MacAdam was born in Scotland in 1756, and while still a young man made a considerable amount of money in America. Upon his return to Great Britain, he took an interest in the improvement of local roads and later became a surveyor responsible for the improvement of road surfaces in the Bristol area. Many in other areas were impressed by the success of MacAdam's methods and asked him to supervise their roads as well.

His methods were simple. MacAdam built his roads of small, light stones, mainly of the sort which would crumble to fill cracks, laid on the ordinary subsoil of the area. Simple though this sounds it was original and effective at the time. MacAdam proved a worthy successor to two pioneer road builders, Jack Metcalf and Thomas Telford. Metcalf was totally blind, yet in 1765 he constructed a road between Harrogate and Boroughbridge using the revolutionary process of laying broken stones instead of the smooth pebbles usually used.

Metcalf's broken stones linked into one another and were not moved by traffic passing over them; a great improvement on the old method.

Thomas Telford, a Scot like MacAdam, built hundreds of miles of roads, adapting and improving on Metcalf's methods. He also constructed canals, but the innovator in this field was Thomas Brindley who became the greatest canal engineer of his time. The canals built by men like Brindley and John Smeaton were used by manufacturers for moving goods all over the country.

By the end of the 18th century Great Britain was firmly launched as an industrial nation. Many different trades and manufacturing business were thriving. These industries were demanding new inventions to help them, and were willing to pay inventors who could come up with the right ideas.

Further Reading

Larsen, *A History of Invention* (Dent)
Kay, *Pioneers of British Industry* (Rockliff)
Dickinson, *James Watt* (Cambridge)
Brearly, *Steelmakers* (Longmans)
Unstead, *The Rise of Great Britain* (Black)
Millward, *The 18th Century* (Hulton)
Harrison, *The 18th Century: a Picture-Source Book* (Allen and Unwin)
Dymoke, *London in the 18th Century* (Longmans)

4 Inventions and Communication

Printing

We have seen how Gutenberg invented his printing machine with movable type and made it possible for large quantities of books to be printed. For some hundreds of years there were few changes made to the German's methods of printing, but there were a number of changes in the things that were printed.

Newspapers became very important. There had been newspapers of a sort before the invention of printing. The Romans had put up news sheets called *acta diurna* in public places, but only a small proportion of the population ever saw what was written upon them.

With the invention of printing it was possible to publish hundreds and even thousands of copies of newspapers and sell them at a profit. One of the first to be issued was in Venice in the 16th century when the government printed a sheet

22 The forerunners of today's newspapers were the news-sheets of the seventeenth century. The vendor here is selling the *London Gazette*, one of the best known of news-sheets. As time went on, however, the news-sheets often tended to be lurid and sensational in order to maintain their circulation.

containing items of news. It was sold for a coin called a gazeta, and this is why we call some newspapers gazettes.

In Great Britain the first news sheets to contain news and information were published in the form of ballads, which were poems about events of the day. Other printed items were small pamphlets containing information. Sometimes a man or group of men would write a pamphlet attacking the government and publish it, much to the annoyance of the people being insulted.

The term 'newspaper' does not seem to have been used before 1670, but the first real newspaper to be issued in Great Britain was almost certainly *The Oxford Gazette*. This was first issued in 1665 and later changed its name to *The London Gazette*.

In addition to newspapers and ballads, books continued to be published and read by the section of the population which could read. One of the most popular of the books printed in the early part of the 18th century was Daniel Defoe's *Robinson Crusoe*, which was published in 1719. This adventure of a man shipwrecked and forced to rely on his wits to survive was very popular and made its author famous. All the same, Defoe's career is an example of how dangerous it could be to criticize political or religious policies. In 1702 he had published a pamphlet entitled 'The Shortest Way With the Dissenters' which got him into trouble with the law, and caused him to be imprisoned and placed in the pillory.

With the increasing public demand for newspapers, publishers started looking for ways of improving printing processes. The introduction of steam as a means of powering the machines made a great help; presses driven by steam could produce more pamphlets in a quicker time than was possible by the old methods.

A man who was very interested in the potential of steam-driven printing machines was a German printer named Friedrich Konig. Konig made a number of experiments and then invented a printing process which was to speed things up even more. His machine was steam-driven. Later he developed a machine that printed on both sides of the sheet in one operation, which meant that the sheets of paper could be printed much more quickly than had been possible before.

Konig was backed and encouraged by an English publisher, John Walter. Walter purchased two of these machines and in 1814 used one of them for printing copies of his newspaper *The Times*. Printers of this newspaper were afraid that they would be put out of work by the new process, and Walter had to print the first edition almost in secret. Later, however, the printers realised that Konig's machine saved a great deal of labour and made their job much easier.

Other improvements followed. In 1863, William Bullock, an American, invented the rotary press. This printed on one huge sheet of paper which could later be divided up into pages and did away with the time-consuming practice of feeding individual pages into the printing machine. Unfortunately, Bullock lost his life falling into one of his own presses. Another great advance in printing occurred in 1886 when Ottmar Mergenthaler finally succeeded in developing a method of setting type by machine instead of by hand. With Mergenthaler's

23 In 1886 the linotype composing machine revolutionised the printing industry. Up to that time type had to be set by hand, a very laborious process. While the new invention did not set type it did make lines of type metal, called slugs, which could be used either for direct printing or for making moulds. The machine in the picture is the one designed by Otto Mergenthaler, known as the 'Blower' Linotype.

process, the type setter sat at a small machine which did mechanically what previously had to be performed laboriously by hand.

Mergenthaler's method of printing was known as linotype printing. He developed a machine, operated by a keyboard, which meant that whole lines of type could be set at once. In printing processes requiring speed, like the production of newspapers, this was a great advantage. The other main type of printing, monotype, was invented by Tolbert Lanston, an American. This was a complicated machine which set a single printed character at a time, a much slower operation than that of the linotype machine.

Both types of printing machine were patented by their inventors. Patenting had become a very important part of industry and its inventions. If an inventor has patented an invention it means that he has registered it at the official government office and that the process belongs to him. If his invention has been patented no one can steal it or its name from the inventor.

By the end of the 19th century enormous advances had been made in printing. Books, magazines and newspapers could be printed and illustrated mechanically. In many parts of Europe and the United States, education became available for more and more people. Before the end of the 19th century a great many men, women and children could read. There was a demand for school text books and for popular reading books and newspapers. The improved printing presses were capable of meeting this demand.

Cameras and Moving Pictures
From the time of Archimedes scientists and inventors had been interested in the subject of optics, which means sight and what we see, and is particularly concerned with mirrors, lenses and reflections.

Archimedes had made experiments with large mirrors, hoping to be able to catch the rays of the sun and deflect them on to the Roman ships, thus setting them on fire. He failed in his ambition, but a thousand years later, in about 1000 A.D., an Arabian scientist called Alhazen carried the experiments of Archimedes a stage further, doing more work with mirrors and reflections.

Leonardo da Vinci was as interested in optics as he was in almost every other branch of science. He and inventors who followed him did a great deal of work in developing what we know as the *camera obscura*. This means *darkened room,* and it consisted of a box with a hole in it. By peering through the hole it was possible to see an image of the scene outside the box.

An inventor who did a great deal to improve the *camera obscura* in the 16th century was a Venetian, Daniello Barbaro, but even before his work we are given a picture of the results of this process in a book published in 1535 by Giambattista della Porta:

> ... in a dark chamber by white sheets objected, one may see as clearly and perspicuously as if they were before his eyes, Huntings, Banquets, Armies of Enemies, Plays and all things else that one desireth.

In 1601 a German, Athanasius Kircher, invented the forerunner of the slide projector when he displayed a crude machine capable of projecting hand made pictures on to a screen. This terrified the onlookers and the German was accused of being a friend of the devil. His work was taken a stage further over 200 years later when John Paris invented the thaumatrope, a toy consisting of a disc rather like a spinning top with a figure drawn on either side. By twirling the thaumatrope the figures seemed to move and form patterns.

By the early part of the 19th century a number of inventors were working on the problem of producing pictures and reflections. One of these men was Thomas Wedgwood, son of the potter. He joined Sir Humphry Davy, inventor of the

24 The principles of the *camera obscura* have been known for centuries. The portable type shown here was once popular with travelling showmen. Light rays enter a small hole in a dark box. They throw, upside down, a reduced picture of the scene outside on to the wall of the box opposite the hole. Zahn, a German monk, improved on this by inserting an optical lens into the aperture; this turned the picture the right way up and made it much more defined.

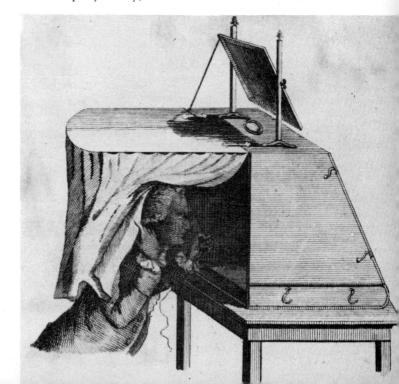

miner's safety lamp, in a number of experiments. They attempted to reproduce pictures by artificial means. They searched for a method of copying paintings on glass and, in their own words, 'of making profiles, by the agency of light upon nitrate of silver'.

They could not carry their experiments to a successful conclusion, although they made a number of discoveries. Eleven years later a French inventor, Joseph Niépce, took their work a stage further. After many failures he found that an outline of a picture could be drawn on a metal plate covered with asphalt which had been exposed to the rays of the sun, and that the picture on this plate could be reproduced. This was a complicated process, but it worked. Greatly heartened, Niépce went on with his experiments. In 1822 the inventor produced a crude but recognisable reproduction of an object. He called his method photography.

In 1829 Niépce started working with another Frenchman, Louis Daguerre. Unfortunately Niépce died in 1833, but Daguerre went on working alone. His major discovery was the fact that pictures could be developed on plates coated

25 This daguerrotype was made about 1837 and is the earliest in existence. The daguerrotype process, evolved by the Frenchman, Louis Daguerre, consisted of making a photographic representation of an object by mercury vapour development of silver iodide exposed on a copper plate.

with silver iodide. Daguerre made his discovery almost by accident. Some old plates which had been put away came into contact with drops of mercury from a broken bottle. Daguerre noticed that this caused clear pictures to develop. He made a number of experiments, and as a result came up with his invention, the daguerrotype.

Daguerre's method of photography caused a great stir. It was clumsy, and people sitting for a daguerrotype reproduction had to pose in the sun for thirty minutes while the process worked.

In the same year as Daguerre's invention, 1839, another method of photography was invented by an Englishman, William Fox Talbot. Fox Talbot was a scholar and artist who became interested in the *camera obscura*. He then conducted a number of experiments with silver chloride layers. The drawback here was that his reproductions were reversed—light became dark and dark became light. Fox Talbot did not give up, and eventually he invented the method of photography involving negatives, aided by suggestions from a famous scientist, Sir John Herschel.

Fox Talbot's invention did not catch on as quickly as Daguerre's had done, but eventually it became apparent that his method was more efficient than the Frenchman's. When further developments were made in photography, they were based on the negative-positive process devised by the Englishman, and the daguerrotype fell out of fashion.

Further improvements were made in photography by Maddox and Swan in Great Britain and by George Eastman and his famous Kodak camera in the United States of America. Eastman's camera was simple to use, and it was the proud boast of the manufacturing company that 'You press the button, we do the rest.'

At first photography was used for portrait studies, but then its scope was widened. What probably alerted people to the full potential of this new art were the war photographs sent back from the fighting in the Crimea and the American Civil War. For the first time men and women could see what war was really like, instead of having to rely on drawings and written accounts.

Experiments continued to be made with moving photographs and pictures. In 1824 Peter Roget had written about his theories of moving pictures, and these theories were put into practice by a number of inventors who designed toys with moving pictures, rather like the earlier work of John Paris and his thaumatrope. Some men, however, were not interested in toys but were concerned with the possibilities of inventing a system of real moving pictures.

Joseph Plateau, a Belgian university professor, went blind staring into the sun while conducting experiments. His work was taken up by Eadweard Muybridge. Muybridge went to California and conducted an experiment in which he placed 24 ordinary cameras next to each other to photograph the movements of a race-horse. Even before Muybridge an American called Coleman Sellers had invented a machine which he patented as the kinematoscope. This consisted of six photographs mounted on a wheel which was rotated to give the impression that the pictures were moving.

Thomas Edison, of whom we shall hear more later, made a number of experiments with moving pictures and invented a machine called a kinetoscope, a sort of peep show in which individuals paid a coin to see pictures whirling round. Edison's idea was developed by an Englishman, Pobert Paul. By 1896 Paul had actually made some short films.

Perhaps the most famous of the Europeans who worked on inventing a moving picture camera was William Friese-Greene. He patented a camera in 1889 and took moving pictures of scenes in Hyde Park in London, but his camera was not as good as one designed by two French brothers called Lumière. In 1895 these two men opened the first cinema in the world in Paris. A great new industry was about to begin, thanks to the efforts of a number of inventors.

Railways

The term 'communication', which we have used as the heading for this chapter, also means methods of travelling from one place to another. From the 18th century onwards men were to make many inventions which improved methods of travelling.

The idea of using fixed rails for vehicles had occurred to men hundreds of years before the first railway locomotives were invented. Primitive men had used wooden runners for their sledges. The first factories had built wooden rails over which trucks could be drawn by horses. With the discovery of new steel smelting processes both rails and the wheels of trucks could be made of iron thus prolonging their life considerably. By 1820 wrought-iron rails, much stronger than the old cast-iron ones, had been developed by John Birkinshaw.

At first these rails were just used in and around factories for transporting raw material and manufactured goods from one part of the factory to another, and from the factory to the nearest road or canal. It soon became apparent that if some sort of powered vehicle could be invented these rails could be extended and used as an efficient means of transport.

The invention of a workable steam engine by James Watt gave a number of inventors the impetus to try and devise a vehicle which would run over the cast-iron rails, especially since a man called Jessop had constructed the cross-section rails which are still used today. Another encouragement for inventors was the fact that many mine owners and industrialists objected to the charges they had to pay Watt for the use of his engine. If someone could invent an engine which he could let the industrialists use cheaply, he might make a lot of money.

Richard Trevithick was one inventor who set out to devise a powered vehicle. He was brought up in Cornwall and was only six years old when the first of Watt's engines was introduced to the tin mines there. When he was 18 Trevithick started work as an engineer in one of the mines.

Almost at once he began work in his spare time, trying to invent his own engine, to the annoyance of Watt and his partners. By 1800, however, Watt's patent, or right to be the only man to manufacture steam engines, expired. Anyone could try to invent his own engine. Trevithick was one of the first to do so. After a number of failures he built what was known as 'Dick's firedragon'. This was a 'car' driven by steam. It was tried out on Christmas Eve, 1801.

To his delight the car worked. The engine actually drove the vehicle up a steep hill. Overjoyed, Trevithick and his friends went off for a drink. Unfortunately they forgot to put out the fire which drove the car's boiler, and the car caught fire and was destroyed.

Trevithick did not give up. He built other steam engines, including another car. In 1804 he invented the first steam locomotive in the world. This ran over rails but proved too heavy, breaking them. Trevithick kept on working. Four years later in 1808 he built another locomotive, one capable of carrying passengers. He brought it to London, hired a patch of ground, put a fence round it

26 Richard Trevithick built the first railway engine in 1804. Here we see the famous locomotive being exhibited in London by the inventor in 1808, ten years before the opening of the first official passenger-carrying line. A large crowd attended this display.

and charged people 1s. a time to ride on his **locom**otive on rails inside the fence. Eventually the rails broke again, causing the locomotive to turn over.

Trevithick had proved that steam-driven locomotives could be built, but other men were to take on his work. Trevithick became ill with typhus and then lost all his money when his business failed. He went abroad to South America, hoping to make a fortune, but had no better luck there. He returned to Great Britain and died in 1833.

A number of inventors followed Trevithick in an effort to perfect a steam-driven vehicle. John Blenkinsop, Matthew Murray and William Hedley all constructed locomotives. The most successful of all, however, was George Stephenson, the son of a stoker. He was to write: 'The strength of Britain lies in her iron and coal beds; and the locomotive is destined, above all other agencies, to bring it forth.'

George Stephenson was born near Newcastle in 1781. He was working at the age of eight, and by nine he was down a mine as a coal sorter. Later he helped to man a Newcomen pump in the pit. He went to evening classes and by sheer determination became an engineer at the Killingworth colliery. Stephenson was commissioned by the mineowner to build a locomotive which would pull trucks full of coal from the mine to the roads and canal. He called the locomotive *Blucher* after a famous Prussian general. It was a success and Stephenson was encouraged to go on making locomotives. Later he was joined by his son Robert, who was to become famous in his own right.

At first there was little interest in railways among the public, but in 1822 George and Robert Stephenson were hired to construct what was in effect to be the first real public railway, a length of line from Stockton to Darlington in the North of England. The work took three years and George Stephenson put all his energies into it. He would travel along the line as it was being constructed, encouraging the workers. One of his colleagues, John Dixon, wrote down one of Stephenson's remarks:

> 'I venture to tell you that I think you will live to see the day when railways will supersede almost all other methods of conveyance in this country— when mail coaches will go by railway, and railroads will become the great highway for the King and all his subjects.'

The Stockton-Darlington line was completed in 1825 and was officially opened on September 17th. George Stephenson himself drove a locomotive along the line, and it was the beginning of passenger and goods traffic on the railways of Great Britain. There were many difficulties to be overcome, but George Stephenson had seen the start of the railway system in this country.

Ships

There had been a number of developments in shipbuilding between the 12th and 17th centuries. Galleys propelled by oars had given way to sailing ships. The invention of the compass in the 14th century enabled vessels to sail farther from land, which in turn led to the construction of larger, stronger ships. In the 19th century, the clippers, the fastest of sailing ships, made the voyage from China to Great Britain in safety.

However, the greatest change was brought about by the introduction of steam. This had as much effect on travel by sea as it had on travel by land. In 1736 Jonathan Hulls had invented a paddle boat powered by a form of steam engine, but could get no financial backing for it. Like many other inventors, Hulls did his work before there was a demand for it. Later, when England desperately needed strong fast vessels in order to export its manufactured goods, any such invention would have stood a better chance of being accepted.

By the beginning of the 19th century, inventors in many countries were trying to develop steam-propelled vessels. In the USA, Rumsey and Fitch were the forerunners of the system. They were followed by a man called Morey and then by Robert Fulton. Fulton was fascinated by anything mechanical and gave up a promising career as an artist in order to become an engineer and inventor. He started by constructing canals, but then James Watt encouraged him to work on designing a steam-driven ship.

The first one that Fulton built was too heavy and sank. Fulton then studied the work of a Scottish engineer, William Symington, who had built a small steamship called the *Charlotte Dundas* and sailed it on the Forth Canal. Fulton then returned to the USA and built his ship, the *Clermont*.

The *Clermont* was a success. In 1807 it steamed 300 miles at four miles an hour up

27 The designs for Robert Fulton's steam-powered paddle boat *Clermont*. Like most inventors Fulton planned his work meticulously, spending hours at the drawing board. When the *Clermont* first appeared, it was an amazing success; in 1807 it steamed 300 miles up the Hudson River at four miles per hour.

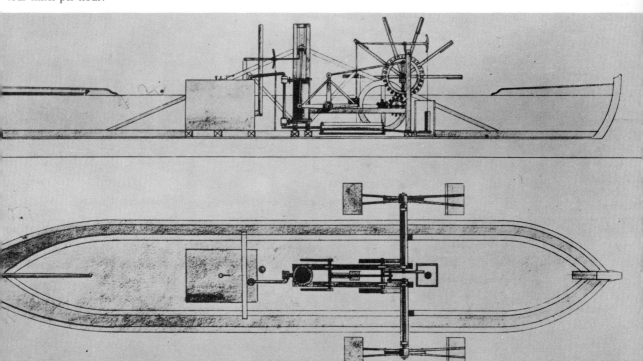

28 The engine room of Brunel's *Great Eastern*. This vessel was 690 feet long and weighed 18,194 tons. Because of its size it had to be launched broadside on. The cost of the launching in 1858 was £120,000, instead of the estimated £14,000, and the owners went bankrupt.

the Hudson River. People were amazed and other inventors strove to build their own steam ships. In Great Britain Henry Bell built the *Comet,* and from 1811 until 1820 it ran regularly between Glasgow and Greenock until it was wrecked in an accident.

From steaming up rivers and across harbours, men set out to cross seas in power-driven ships. In 1813 the *Elizabeth* steamed from Glasgow to Liverpool, driven by an eight horse-power engine. Six years later, the American *Savannah* crossed the Atlantic using sails for much of the journey but powered by a steam engine for about three of the 80 days occupied by the trip. The first steam ship to cross the Atlantic entirely by steam was the Canadian *Royal William* in 1831.

In Great Britain, Isambard Kingdom Brunel wanted to extend the range of the Great Western Railway which he had built. In an effort to do this he built a steamboat called the *Great Western* which crossed the Atlantic for the first time in 1838. The *Great Western* made the crossing in 15 days, beating an American tug by three days.

A further development came about when the screw propeller was invented. A number of men worked independently on this, including Bernouilli from

Switzerland and John Fitch of Great Britain. The idea was taken up by Brunel who used it in several vessels, including the *Great Eastern*, which blew up in an explosion.

With the development of the steam engine and the propeller, shipbuilders began to forsake wood and used first iron and then steel for building their ships.

Roads and Bridges

We have already heard of the road-building exploits of Metcalf, Telford and MacAdam. Men were also constantly concerned with improving the vehicles which had to run on these roads.

From the days of primitive men, with their sledges mounted on runners, people progressed to using horses, oxen and asses. They invented carts on wheels which could be pulled by animals. Merchants of the 15th and 16th centuries carried their goods in baskets strapped on pack-horses. At about this time various forms of coach came into use. There were the huge ponderous road waggons, the horse-sedans for use in towns, and stage coaches like the 'Farnham Fly'.

Inventors also turned their minds to developing powered transport to be used on land. As early as 1680 Sir Isaac Newton had built a model self-propelled steam engine, and he was followed by a Frenchman, Nicholas Cugnot, who, in 1769, built a larger version capable of going at two miles an hour.

Richard Trevithick built his vehicle "Dick's firedragon" in 1801, and a number of other inventors experimented with steam-driven cars. Some of them also considered the possibility of building a car powered by gas. One of these was a Frenchman, Alphonse Beau de Rochas, who developed his first gas-powered vehicle in 1862 and started producing them commercially in 1876.

Other men like Daimler and Benz experimented with various motor cars, but they concentrated at first on gas-powered ones. It was an Englishman, Herbert Ackroyd-Stuart, who invented an engine powered by heavy oil. He was emulated by Rudolph Diesel who developed a workable petrol-driven car in 1897.

Improvements in roads kept pace with the increased amount of traffic travelling over them. Engineers also constructed bridges capable of bearing heavy traffic. Thomas Telford was one prominent bridge-builder. In 1803, he was given the task of improving and building the bridges and roads of the Highlands of Scotland. He did this with great efficiency, constructing almost 1,000 miles of road and 1,117 bridges. Telford was a conscientious man. He took great trouble over the construction of his roads and bridges and they were not cheap. When they were completed, however, both bridges and roads were firm and strong.

With the development of iron, bridges were constructed of this material and Telford built one magnificent iron bridge over the Menai Straits between the mainland and Anglesey. Robert Stephenson also used iron for the construction of bridges when he was building his railway lines across the north of England, while Isambard Brunel constructed a fine bridge of wrought iron at Saltash.

29 *Left (above)* The first gas-powered Benz car, designed and built in 1886. The first 'automobile', built by Cugnot in France in 1769, was steam-driven. But steam-powered cars were penalised in the mid-nineteenth century by a number of laws which made it difficult to put such vehicles on the road. Other means of propulsion were therefore sought. Men like Benz experimented with gas engines, but eventually the internal combustion engine of the sort patented by Daimler in 1885 *(below)* won the day.

30 *Below* Otto Lilienthal in his glider in 1896. It was Lilienthal who inspired the Wright brothers to conduct the experiments which led to the first heavier-than-air flight. Lilienthal's one-man gliders were quite successful – until the inventor himself met his death on one flight.

Air Travel

Pioneers were also experimenting with machines which they hoped would fly. Some of them built wings of feathers in an attempt to imitate birds, and threw themselves from mountain-tops and other high places. Most of them crashed and were killed or badly hurt.

The earliest successful bids to fly were made by men in balloons. The first to claim to have done so was a monk called Gusamao in 1708, but it was not until 1783 that two Frenchmen, the Montgolfier brothers, built a balloon which really worked. Their first flight with human passengers took place on 21 November, 1783.

Two other brothers, German this time, called Otto and Gustav Lilienthal, were the next successful aviators. They made many attempts to invent a flying machine. Otto later wrote about their theories, saying:

> The observation of flying creatures shows that it is possible by means of peculiarly-shaped wings, which are moved through the air in a definite manner, to maintain heavy bodies floating in the air. . . .

The flying machine, which was really a forerunner of the glider, invented by the Lilienthals, consisted of one large pair of wings and two smaller pairs. They propelled it into the air by running down a hill and leaping into the air. In this fashion they made several short flights. Their work inspired many other inventors to try and develop flying machines, and even when Otto Lilienthal was killed in a flying accident it did not stop other men continuing their work. The time was not far off when the Wright brothers would fly their heavier-than-air machine.

Further Reading

Begg-Humphries, *The Industrial Revolution* (Allen and Unwin)
Sambrook (ed.), *English Life in the 19th Century* (Macmillan)
Boumphrey, *Engines and How they Work* (Studio Vista)
Herbert, *Over to You, the story of communications* (Brockhampton)
Hogben, *Men, Missiles and Machines* (Rathbone)
Salter, *Great Moments in Engineering* (Phoenix House)
Styles, *The Battle of Steam* (Constable)
Pannell, *Illustrated History of Civil Engineering* (Thames and Hudson)
Knight, *The Liveliest Art, a Panoramic History of the Movies* (Mentor)
Griffith and Mayer, *The Movies* (Spring Books)

5   Inventions and Men's Jobs

Farm Workers

Improved communications meant that farm livestock and produce could be transported from the country to the market towns and ports much more easily than had been the case before. This meant that farm owners found more buyers for their goods.

Inventions which made farmers more prosperous were those like the seed drill perfected by Jethro Tull. This drill penetrated the earth deeply, because Tull believed that the roots of crops should be fed as they grew. His method made farming more efficient because the soil was broken up and the crops planted in straight rows, which made it both possible for crops to be grown in soil hitherto too stiff and solid for planting, and also to be gathered in easily as the grain grew in the rows in which the seeds were planted. Strong horses were needed to pull Tull's drill and this led to the special breeding of big, strong horses.

At first it was only the farm owners who benefited from such inventions; like their counterparts in the towns and cities, farm workers believed that these new developments would put them out of work. Some of them tried to destroy the drills manufactured by Tull's process; others refused to use them. Eventually the workers came to realise that these instruments were designed to make their jobs easier, but it took some time before they were accepted. The same was true

31 Jethro Tull did much to aid the resurgence of English farming in the early part of the eighteenth century. He studied the growth of plants and tried to make a science out of agriculture. This picture shows his mechanical seed drill which dug the trenches for the seeds, dropped them from a box and covered them with earth as it went along.

of new methods developed by such farming pioneers as Lord Townshend, Robert Bakewell and Thomas Coke.

Similar doubts were expressed when other inventions to help farmers came on the market. In America Cyrus McCormick invented a corn reaping machine; this was drawn by horses, but cut and bundled the stalks mechanically. Across the Atlantic in Great Britain the firm of J. R. and A. Ransome designed and built a primitive traction engine powered by steam. It still needed a horse to guide it, but in 1842, the year of its invention, this was a revolutionary machine for threshing corn.

Another advance was made by John Fowler of Wiltshire, who invented the first workable steam-powered plough. However, it was the inventors like Nicholas Otto, experimenting with petrol-driven machines, who made the greatest contribution to farm mechanisation. The developments of men like Otto and William Maybach were adapted for use on the land by Dan Albone, a Bedfordshire man, who in 1902 invented a petrol driven motor tractor which proved very successful.

The farmworkers were still dubious about the mechanical aids being introduced throughout the 19th century. At the same time many of them were leaving the land for employment in the factories, where more money could be earned. This meant that there were less workers on the land to do even more work, as the demand for food was increasing. The new inventions made it possible for fewer men to do more work; in this way they were accepted.

Factory Workers

The new inventions made a considerable difference to the jobs of men and women working in factories. Factories had been in existence long before the 18th century; there is a poem about a 16th century cloth-making factory, part of which runs:

> Within one roome being large and long
> There stood two hundred Loomes full strong:
> Two hundred men the truth is so
> Wrought in these Loomes all in a row.

Even so, the inventions of the 18th and 19th centuries changed the factories and the lives of those who worked in them. New processes were introduced by the factory owners. This was particularly true of the iron and steel foundries. One example was Henry Cort's iron manufacturing process. When water power had been used to power a large hammer, it took 12 hours to produce one ton of iron bars. Cort experimented with coal fuel and a device known as a rolling mill to produce 15 tons in the same period of time. This meant that other processes in the factory had to be speeded up to keep up with the rolling mill.

Another man who altered the lives of factory workers was Henry Bessemer. He invented a furnace in which blasts of hot air were forced through molten

32 Grinding and polishing in an eighteenth-century factory. Mechanisation, in an elementary form, was slowly beginning to creep into the manufacture of weapons.

33 It was Henry Bessemer who first discovered a method of mass-producing cheap steel. He discovered that directing a current of air through a mass of molten iron produced a metal stronger than any other then known. This picture shows the foundry he built for the large-scale construction of this steel.

metal, thus clearing it of impurities. As a result the quality of steel was improved, but the labourers working near these furnaces had a hot and uncomfortable task.

We have heard how many workers distrusted inventors and did their best to destroy the machines which they thought would put them out of work. In some cases their fears were justified, but as a rule the new inventions meant more work as long as there was a demand for manufactured goods. Even this was not an unmixed blessing. Thousands of workers left the country to come and work in the towns. For the first time England became a country in which more people worked in industry than on the land. This meant that the towns and cities became overcrowded and that the poorly paid workers had to live in conditions of considerable squalor.

In this new age of machinery the craftsmanship of the older skilled workers began to disappear as the new demand was for quantity, not for individual precision work. On the other hand, however, the tools that were being developed made it possible for unskilled workers to attain higher standards of production. Maudslay always set an example in the correct use of tools. One workman said of him:'It was a pleasure to see him handle a tool of any kind, but he was quite splendid with an eighteen inch file.'

Thanks to the new inventions some workers found themselves doing jobs they had never attempted before. Few had quite the experience that befell a coachman working for Sir George Cayley, who was one of the pioneers in aircraft invention in about 1852. It is said that eventually he succeeded in making an aeroplane that actually flew a few hundred yards, with the unfortunate coachman in it. The primitive machine crashed and the coachman staggered out of the wreckage and approached Sir George Cayley saying, with great dignity: 'Please, Sir George, I wish to give notice. I was hired to drive and not to fly.'

Many industrialists made great fortunes out of their factories, and owed much of their success to the inventions which powered the factories. Even so, it was not entirely the profit motive which urged men on to invent more machines and appliances; many had a vision of a great future in which inventions like the power of flight would make the world a richer and happier place. The poet Tennyson, writing in the 19th century, dreamt of a time when aeroplanes would carry goods from one country to another:

> For I dipt into the future, far as human eye could see,
> Saw the Vision of the world, and all the wonder that would be;
> Saw the heavens fill with commerce, argosies of magic sails,
> Pilots of the purple twilight, dropping down with costly bales;

With more and more men working in factories they were pressed together to a greater extent than ever before. For the first time many of them had a chance to talk to other workers in large numbers, and after a time these workmen realised that they could best look after their own interests if they stuck together. From these early meetings the great trade unions of the latter part of the 19th and early 20th centuries began.

34 A once-familiar sight in London – the gathering of mail coaches at St Martin's-le-Grand. By 1820 there was an extensive collection of coach routes across the country and many different kinds of coach were found on these roads. It was the heyday of road transport – before the railways were seen to have commercial possibilities.

Making Life Easier

Many of the new inventions went a long way to making life easier and more convenient for people in the 19th century. The improved roads and coach designs made it possible for mail to get from one part of the country to another with much more speed than had been the case before. Passengers, too, could travel the length and breadth of the land. Writing in 1830 a man pointed out that:

> In the present day, a journey from Edinburgh to London is a matter at once safe, brief and simple, however inexperienced or unprotected the traveller. Numerous coaches of different rates of charge, and as many packets, are perpetually passing and repassing betwixt the capital of Britain and her northern sister, so that the most timid or indolent may execute such a journey upon a few hours' notice.

Other developments made home life pleasanter. The introduction of gas lighting, improvements in household furniture and appliances, the introduction of cheaper and more effective ways of making glass and other tableware, the adaptation of printing for better text-books in schools, all helped to make life comfortable for the middle and upper classes. The poorer people still lived in unpleasant and unhealthy conditions, but even they were to benefit from the improvements to come.

Further Reading

Bellis, *Britain in a Changing World* (Cassell)
Briggs, *The Age of Improvement* (Longmans)
Addy, *The Agrarian Revolution* (Longmans)
Boyce, *Tools and Machines* (Macmillan)

6   Inventions and Men's Health

The Medical Profession

Most developments in the medical profession owed more to the efforts of scientific research workers than to inventors, but a number of inventions made the work of doctors and surgeons less complicated.

Medicine needs tools. This seems to have been recognised 30,000 years ago. Skulls dating back to this time have been found containing holes obviously made by primitive stone tools. These brain operations must have been carried out with stone scalpels, forerunners of the delicate instruments used today.

More intricate operations were being carried out by surgeons in the Middle East 4,000 years ago. A code of fees and penalties was laid down for some of these doctors, one of which read:

> If a doctor shall treat a gentleman and shall open an abscess with a bronze knife or shall preserve the eye of the patient, he shall receive ten shekels of silver.

By the 5th century A.D. Indians had invented many medical instruments, including saws, probes, forceps and lancets. These instruments spread to Europe, where they were used by doctors.

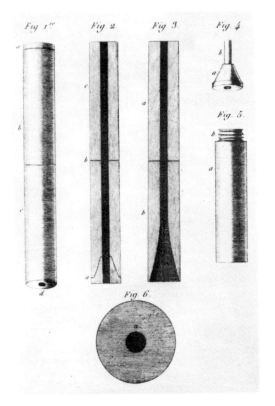

35   A diagram of the parts of René Laennec's stethoscope. This is far removed from the delicate instrument used by doctors today but at the time of its invention it revolutionised diagnostic medicine.

36 Roentgen's work on X-ray apparatus was responsible for an immense step forward in medical science. Roentgen discovered while working with an electric current that if he placed a metal plate in the path of a cathode stream, the penetrating rays were made much more powerful. The apparatus here was in use in 1897; notice the hand in position on the photographic plate.

By the 18th century, more sophisticated apparatus was being developed. An Italian, Luigi Galvani, invented the galvanometer which used the principle of electricity to shock or galvanise animals into movement. His work was later used for stimulating the brains of men injured at the Battle of Sedan in 1870.

A great stride forward was made in the 19th century by a Frenchman called René Laennec. Laennec invented the stethoscope, the instrument used by doctors for listening to the heart. Before Laennec's invention they had been forced to listen by placing their ears to the chests of their patients.

Another invention, this time devised in America, was a crude machine in the form of a rubber bag and a tube for administering gas to a patient in order to render him insensible during an operation. The gas—termed 'laughing gas'—had been discovered by Sir Humphry Davy in Great Britain, but was first used on a large scale in 1832 by Gardner Colton, a travelling showman, who drew large crowds in America by demonstrating the effects of this gas. His idea was taken up by a dentist, Horace Wells. Wells used the gas-filled rubber bag and tube to render patients unconscious while he removed their teeth. Other doctors adapted and improved upon Wells's device, and the science of anaesthetics was under way.

Other instruments were not slow in being developed. The ophthalmoscope for studying the eyes was invented, as was the laryngoscope for the examination of the throat. But perhaps the most important of all 19th century medical inventions was the X-ray machine.

This was invented by a Bavarian physicist, Wilhelm Roentgen. During the course of some experiments on fluorescence he discovered that if he placed a tube containing barium-platino-cyanide crystals in a darkened container and passed an electric current through an electrode at the mouth of the tube, the contents of the tube could be seen glowing through the container. From this discovery Roentgen went on to build the first X-ray machine. His work was taken up by other inventors and researchers and another significant step forward in the science of medicine had been taken.

Public Health

A number of inventions were responsible for a great improvement in public health and sanitation.

One of the chief hazards to health in towns and cities has always been impure water supplies. City authorities seem to have been aware of this from early times and to have sought for ways of purifying the water in their midst. The obvious way of doing this was by pumping water in and out of the cities, thus preventing it from stagnating. In 1578, in England, Peter Morris, a mining engineer, was conducting experiments with water pumps. His skill in designing a water pump is referred to in a contemporary report:

> Peter Morris hath by his great labour and charge found out and learned the skill and coning to make some new kynde and manner of engynes to draw up waters higher than nature yt selfe.

Morris's pump gave London a supply of fresh water from the Thames. In 1767 another pumping system was introduced by John Smeaton, but it was Joseph Bramah with his hydraulic press who provided enough pumping power in the 19th century for water closets to be built in houses some way from the river, and on the upper storeys of some houses.

37 Peter Morris designed this water pump in the late seventeenth century to give London an efficient supply of fresh water. It was one of the earliest attempts to overcome the dreadful public health hazards that stemmed from unclean water in overcrowded cities. Several of the early steam engines were also designed with this idea partly in mind.

Ah! this is what comes of Improvement — this is the happy effects of the March of Intellect — No employment for Scavengers now — when I had the management of the Rubbish concern, I found plenty of employment for all of them.

New Machine for Sweeping Streets Invented by Col. Boaze

Pub. by S. Gans 15 Southampton St Strand May 16 1829

38 The innovation of machines for cleaning city streets is here made the subject of a political cartoon, with Lord Eldon as the cleaner. It is interesting to see the implication that the introduction of machinery is a threat to men's jobs. Lord Eldon is commenting that the horse-drawn cleaning apparatus is even putting the lowly scavengers out of work.

Other pioneers began to devise ways of keeping the ever growing towns and cities healthy. A man called Whitworth invented a road-sweeping machine. John Roe, a 19th century surveyor, designed a system for flushing and cleaning sewers. Edwin Chadwick, a public health official, drew up plans for an efficient drainage system. Such plans were badly needed. Fifty-four people signed a letter appearing in *The Times* on 5 July, 1849:

Sur

May we beg and beseach your proteckshion and power. We are Sur, as it may be, livin in a Wilderness, so far as the rest of London knows anything of us, or the rich and great people care about. We live in muck and filthe. We aint got no priviz, no dust bins, no drains, no water splies, and no drain or suer in the whole place. The Suer Company, in Greek Street, Soho

Square, all great, rich and powerfool men, take no notice watsomedever of our cumplaints. The Stench of a Gully-hole is disgustin. We al of us suffur, and numbers are ill, and if the Colera comes Lord help us. . . .

Home Comforts

While the poor were living in great discomfort in the 19th century, a number of inventions made life more convenient and pleasant for those able to afford them.

One of these advances was in the field of time-telling. By the middle of the 19th century the clock and watch-maker's art had been brought to a high standard. Accurate time-keeping had been greatly improved when Huygens developed the pendulum as applied to clocks in 1657. Another invention in the 17th century was Robert Hooke's use of the spring in the balance of watches. Other inventors were not slow to recognise the importance of a delicate watch spring to provide accurate time-keeping, and Hooke's work was advanced by Abraham Bregeut, and in 1860 by Edouard Phillips.

New materials, too, were being developed to make people's lives healthier and more comfortable. Materials like nickel, cobalt and aluminium were extracted for the first time in the 19th century. Rubber, discovered in the jungles of Brazil, became an important commodity when Hancock in England and Goodyear in the USA discovered how to process and manufacture it. In 1867 Hyatt invented celluloid and in 1888 J. B. Dunlop improved on the earlier work of people like the Scot, Thomson, and invented the pneumatic tyre.

By the end of the 19th century people were no longer frightened by the new inventions surrounding them. They were beginning to accept and make use of them.

Further Reading
Burstall, *A History of Mechanical Engineering* (Faber)
Dunsheath, *A Century of Technology* (Hutchinson
Edwards-Rees, *The Story of Nursing* (Constable)
Cuss, *The Story of Watches* (Macgibbon and Kee)

7 The Use Made of Inventions

During the last years of the 19th century and for the first decade or so of the 20th century, men seemed to concentrate on developing and putting to more effective use the inventions already patented. There were still many new discoveries, but most technological work seemed to stem either from work already done or as a direct result of a need for improvements in the new industries being established. lished.

Transport

Railways in Great Britain had started with a tragic accident when William Huskisson, a Member of Parliament, had been knocked down and killed by the *Rocket* at the ceremonial opening of the Manchester-Liverpool line in 1830. However, even this could not prevent the progress of railways. Men like Robert Stephenson and Isambard Brunel built better and better locomotives and more efficient railway lines. Industrialists poured money into them by opening railway companies like the Great Western and the London and North Eastern.

The development of the railways owed much to the engineers who perfected ways of building bridges and tunnels. Brunel did much bridge construction using wrought iron, while Hodgkinson and Fairbairn attracted the support of Robert Stephenson with their tubular bridges. Later, the processes of Bessemer led to the mass production of cheap steel which could be used for railway lines and bridges.

Other developments followed. In 1859 the first railway sleeping car was introduced in the USA by George Pullman. Ten years later George Westinghouse developed a system of brakes powered by compressed air. In 1890 corridors appeared on trains for the first time in Great Britain, which was an added convenience for passengers. By 1880 trains were already travelling at high speeds,

39 Brunel's suspension bridge at Clifton, a triumph of engineering.

and they were to change little until steam locomotives were replaced by trains using different forms of power many years later.

Railway locomotives seemed to reach an acceptable standard of performance within quite a short time. The same could not be said of motor cars, which went through many transformations. At first it appeared as if steam-driven cars would be the most suitable means of road transport, but then Daimler and Benz started making their experiments with the petrol-driven internal combustion engine.

In France, the Marquis de Dion and others led the way, but in Great Britain the pioneers were men like Harry Lawson, Henry Sturmey and F. R. Simms. Many people laughed at these early vehicles, but a few realised that what the railways had started, motor cars might finish, namely the end of the supremacy of the horse as a means of transport. One manufacturing firm of the time called itself the Great Horseless Carriage Company. Embittered farmers complained that if these carriages did indeed replace horses, there would eventually be no manure left with which to fertilise the fields.

Inventors turned their talents to producing additional mechanical aids for cars. The three Lanchester brothers invented cars with such refinements as wire wheels and rudimentary gear boxes. Henry Royce, financed by C. S. Rolls, produced the famous Rolls Royce car. Dunlop's pneumatic tyres made motoring more comfortable.

40 On the assembly line at an early Ford factory each man had only a limited number of functions. He performed the same service on every car that came before him. Ford's idea was later taken a stage further by the introduction of moving assembly belts which propelled the complete assembly down a line of workmen, each performing the same mechanical task again and again.

Until 1896, any car driving on the roads of Great Britain had to be preceded by a man walking ahead carrying a red flag. This was abolished by an Act of Parliament, and motorists were free to drive at speed. In the USA, the production of cars became a major industry at the beginning of the 20th century, thanks mainly to the efforts of Henry Ford. Ford was a good mechanic, but his main contribution to the industry was the design of the assembly-line. In his factories mass-production was utilised to build fifteen million Ford cars in 20 years. With the coming of the First World War in 1914, motoring was on its way to becoming one of the most important industries in the world.

Another popular means of transport was the bicycle. It was developed in France. The French forerunner of the bicycle was the hobby horse. This consisted of a saddle attached to a cross bar and two wooden wheels. The rider propelled himself along with his feet. The hobby horse was followed by the penny farthing bicycle, one large wheel and a small one, surmounted by a saddle.

With the coming of cheaper steel and the invention of the pneumatic tyre in about 1888, inventors designed a bicycle which, although very heavy, was closer in appearance to the ones we see today. The comparative cheapness of the vehicles made cycling a popular sport as well as a means of transport. There were also efforts to make roller-skating a general means of transport, and there was a brief vogue for it at the end of the 19th century, but this was not maintained and it became merely a spare-time activity.

During the period 1880–1918 Great Britain possessed the largest and most powerful navy in the world. The most important development in ship building in the latter part of the 19th century was Sir Charles Parsons' invention of the marine steam turbine. This was fitted to a number of vessels, including the destroyer *Viper* which was able to travel at a speed of 37 knots.

The most rapid advances in transport, however, came in air travel. After the efforts of the Lilienthal brothers many inventors set to work, some copying the gliders developed by the Lilienthals, others striving to invent a flying machine heavier than air and powered by an engine.

Two young American mechanics, Orville and Wilbur Wright, were among the inventors who set out to build a heavier-than-air flying machine. In their early days the two men worked at a variety of trades, but eventually they opened a small bicycle factory. They then settled down to their experiments. At first they designed gliders, but soon turned to designing aeroplanes powered by engines. In 1899, Wilbur Wright wrote a letter in which he expressed his determination to discover as much as he could about flight:

> I am about to begin a systematic study of the subject in preparation for practical work to which I expect to devote what time I can spare from my regular business.

The two brothers carried out their trials at Kittyhawk in North Carolina. They housed their aeroplane in a shed while they lived in a tent. They had to survive a number of disasters. A storm almost blew their aeroplane away, the

41 The Wright brothers were the first men to fly successfully in a heavier-than-air machine. We see here Orville at the controls and Wilbur looking on. They added a petrol engine to a modified version of a glider and made the historic flight on 17 December 1903.

engine began to give trouble, various things went wrong with other parts of the machine. After a number of experiments with a steam engine, the brothers built one powered by petrol and used that.

Finally, on 17 December 1903, they were ready to attempt their flight. They invited people in the neighbourhood to come and watch their effort to make history. Only four men and a boy bothered to turn up. Nevertheless, the Wrights went on with their flight. On a cold December morning Orville Wright made the first sustained flight in a machine heavier than air. Later he was to give his own account of what had happened:

> The first flight lasted only twelve seconds, a very short time in comparison with the flight of a bird, but it was nevertheless the first time in the history of the world in which a machine carrying a man had raised itself by its own power into the air in full flight, had sailed forward without reduction of speed, and had finally landed at a point as high as that from which it had started.

Between them Orville and Wilbur Wright made four flights that morning at Kittyhawk. Then a gust of wind seized the aeroplane while it was still on the ground, and overturned it, injuring one of the spectators.

The Wrights gave a number of demonstrations of their flying machine. At first the public showed little interest, but other inventors realised the importance of the first flight of a heavier-than-air machine. Other men began to build and fly their own powered aeroplanes. The aircraft industry was about to begin.

In Europe inventors were slow to follow the Wright brothers, but in 1906

Albertos Santos-Dumont, a Brazilian working in France, made a flight of almost two hundred feet. Other men were working on engined aircraft in Great Britain, but writing in *The Times* in 1906 an editor said, 'all attempts at artificial aviation are not only dangerous to human life, but foredoomed to failure from the engineering standpoint.'

It was a view shared by others, but not by the engineers and inventors working on their machines. Men like Verdon Roe, Samuel Cody and other pioneers went on experimenting in spite of set-backs and ridicule. The final breakthrough came in the USA when the Army ordered a number of flying machines to be built by the Wright brothers. With this official backing the two brothers were able to go ahead and design better and more powerful machines.

Communications

After the experiments of Edison, Friese-Greene and Paul, and the opening of the world's first cinema by the Lumière brothers in 1895, the film industry attracted a great deal of interest among inventors and financiers willing to put up the money for further experiments.

Films began to be shown at music halls. There is an account of one such showing in New York in 1896, by a reporter for *The New York Times*:

> . . . an unusually bright light fell upon the screen. Then came into view two precious blond persons of the variety stage, in pink and blue dresses, doing the umbrella dance with commendable celerity. . . .

Among the brilliant men who invented the basic technical tricks of cinema-photography was a Frenchman called Georges Melies. By 1900 he had discovered ways of using the camera in order to produce short films containing slow and fast motion photography, as well as many other technical devices still being used today, including a form of cartoon or animated film. The public became fascinated by this new form of entertainment. By the beginning of the 20th century, films were moving from the music halls to specially constructed cinemas.

In 1903, an American company produced the first film to contain a story. Before that films had usually been scenes of different events, like a train arriving at a station, people leaving a factory, and so on. The American film was called *The Great Train Robbery*, and it was very successful. Other companies began making films with actors, and in 1915 a director called D. W. Griffith made a film called *Birth of a Nation*. It lasted almost three hours and attracted huge crowds all over the world.

Although the films of this time were silent, with written sub-titles flashed upon the screen, they became the world's most popular form of entertainment.

Scientists and inventors were also at work on another means of communication —wireless messages. In 1794, a Frenchman, Claud Chappe, had built a rudimentary telegraph line between Paris and Lille. This consisted of a number of poles six miles apart. Each pole had signal arms which could be twisted into

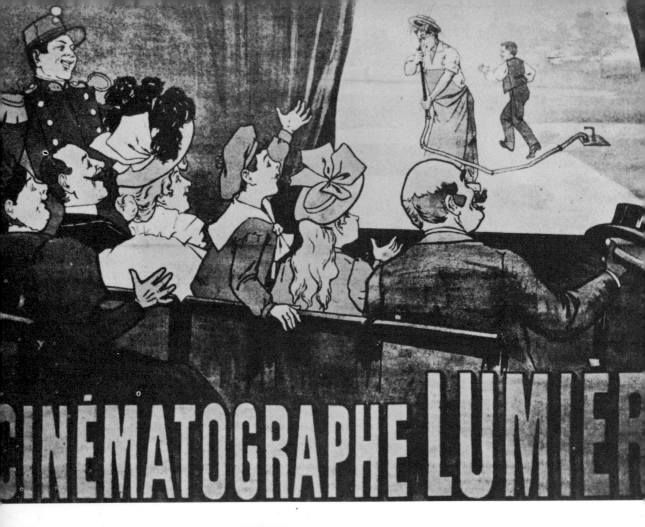

CINÉMATOGRAPHE LUMIÈR

42 *Above* Come to the cinema! This French poster advertises the first moving pictures, exhibited by the Lumière brothers; their all-purpose mechanism filmed moving pictures, and then printed and projected them. The Lumière brothers also standardised the width of film at 35 mm and designed the sprocket holes which are still in use today. They opened the world's first cinema in a Paris basement in 1895.

43 *Left* A scene from 'The Great Train Robbery', made in 1903, and probably the first film to possess a plot. It was a 'Western', lasting 15 minutes, and directed by Edwin S. Porter, an American who had been a camera-man in Thomas Edison's film company.

different positions, each position representing letters and figures. An operator armed with a telescope was situated at each pole, and as he saw a message appearing on the pole next to him he would alter his own signal arms so that the next operator could alter *his* signal, and so on right along the line.

A number of inventors wondered if Chappe's telegraph could be adapted so that messages could be sent from one spot to another by electricity. After a number of experiments a German, Wilhelm Weber, transmitted a message in code using electricity in the year 1833. Eleven years later two British scientists, William Cooke and Charles Wheatstone, built the first telegraph in Great Britain. Another system had also been devised by Edward Davy, a chemist. He developed a telegraph system in 1836 and hoped that the authorities would take over his idea. In fact he wrote in a letter in 1838, 'I think our Government ought, and perhaps will, eventually take it upon themselves as a branch of the Post Office. . . .'

Davy left England to live in Australia, however, and it was the telegraph system invented by Cooke and Wheatstone which was eventually adopted by the General Post Office in Great Britain after a number of experiments by private telegraph companies. The railway companies also adopted the telegraph as a means of communication.

An American, Samuel Morse, made the most important advance in telegraphy. Morse was an artist and it was not until he was over 40 years old that he made the discovery which was to bring him fame. In 1837 he demonstrated the transmitting device known as the Morse key. Later he invented an alphabet consisting of dots and dashes, known as the Morse code, to be transmitted by this key, and this became universally accepted.

In 1850, two brothers in Great Britain called Brett laid the first submarine cable across the English Channel from Dover to Calais. A few words were transmitted over this cable but unfortunately a fishing vessel hooked it to the surface. After numerous attempts another cable was finally laid in 1866.

With telegraphy established as a means of communication some inventors turned their attention to the potentialities of another device—the telephone. In Germany a man called Reis first used electric currents in order to transmit sounds, but it is a Scot, Alexander Graham Bell, who generally receives credit as the inventor of the telephone.

In March 1876, Bell made the first telephone call. He transmitted his voice from one room to another in his house in Boston, saying to his assistant: 'Mr. Watson, come here, I want you.'

A number of people claimed to have invented the telephone before or at the same time as Bell, and several law suits followed; but Bell won them all. In 1877 he formed the Bell Telephone Association. Other inventors like Edison, Blake and Clerac developed refinements to Bell's process and in 1877 the world's first public telephone exchange was opened. At the time of Bell's death in 1922 there were estimated to be 17 million telephones in North America, and millions more

44 Guglielmo Marconi and his wireless apparatus in 1896. Experimenting with electric waves in the air, he invented a form of aerial and a connection to earth. This improved source of power enabled him to transmit and receive signals over a wide distance; by 1901 Marconi had sent radio signals across the Atlantic from Britain to Newfoundland.

overseas. In honour of Bell's memory there was one minute's silence observed over all American telephone lines on the day of the inventor's death.

Scientists and inventors were also busy with the idea of wireless or radio. The first to produce a workable method of utilising radio waves as a means of communication was an Italian, Gugliemo Marconi.

Marconi was born in 1874. Twenty years later, while he was a student at Bologna University, he became interested in an account of experiments carried out on electro-magnetic waves by a German called Heinrich Hertz. Marconi's parents allowed him to work at home on the problems of radio communication, and in 1895 he invented a practical means of transmitting and receiving radio messages over a short distance.

Marconi then moved to England where he carried on with his experiments. The Post Office gave him assistance, and in 1897 he formed a wireless telegraph company. In 1898 he transmitted a radio telegram from the Isle of Wight to Bournemouth, and three years later broadcast a message across the Atlantic Ocean.

By the outbreak of the First World War in 1914, enough progress had been made for people to start thinking about the possibility of opening commercial radio stations to broadcast entertainment and information programmes.

Thomas Edison

Of all the inventors of the 19th and early part of the 20th centuries, the one man to stand head and shoulders above the rest was the American, Thomas Alva Edison.

Even as a boy Edison was experimenting with telegraphy and printing. While still a youth he printed and distributed a newspaper on a train, and engaged in a number of other scientific and technological activities. In a long lifetime he patented literally hundreds of inventions, starting with a machine to count votes and proceeding to the electric light bulb, the kinetoscope, the phonograph, and many others.

Edison was an inventor, not a scientist. He used the findings of scientists to help him arrive at his discoveries, but achieved most of his results by sheer hard work. He once said of himself:

When I am after a chemical result that I have in mind, I may make hundreds or thousands of experiments out of which there may be one that promises results in the right direction. . . .

The first of Edison's major inventions was an improved form of electric light in 1879. Other men before him had made experiments with electricity. In 1752, Benjamin Franklin had experimented by flying a kite in a thunderstorm. When the kite was struck by lightning, Franklin stored the resultant electricity in a special Leyden jar. Galvani, the Italian scientist, experimented with the effects of stimulating animals with electric shocks, and a great deal of work was done by Sir Humphrey Davy and his assistant Michael Faraday.

Edison was familiar with the work done by these men, and the use made of electricity by Samuel Morse when devising his transmitting key. In 1879, after many failures, he invented a long-lasting electric light bulb by putting a thin wire or filament inside a glass bulb. This caused the bulb to glow white hot when a charge of electricity was passing through the wire. Before long, houses and then whole cities were being illuminated by Edison's invention.

Electric light took the place of gas lighting. Illumination by gas had first been developed in Cornwall by William Murdock, and had been taken up on a large scale by commercial firms. The representatives of the gas-lighting industry fought

45 An early carbon filament lamp, lit in an Edison lampholder with an integral switch (about 1884).

the introduction of electric lighting, but could not prevent the new invention superseding the old methods.

Edison later joined forces with Joseph Swan, another inventor, to market an improved electric light bulb, and then went on to other things. In addition to the kinetoscope, he was one of the first men to experiment with talking films. He tried to devise a method of running silent films accompanied by dialogue and sound effects produced by a phonograph, but the experiment was not really a success.

The phonograph was the name Edison gave to his invention of the forerunner of the record player. This consisted of a tubular machine powered by turning a handle. The first words ever recorded on it were those of the inventor as he recited 'Mary had a little lamb. . . .' Edison's ideas were later improved upon

46 Not all inventions were as successful as their inventors hoped! This is Henry Bessemer's saloon steamer, designed to be an anti sea-sickness device; no matter how much the ship swayed or rolled the saloon was supposed to remain on an even keel. In practice this did not happen and the poor occupants of the saloon received a dreadful buffeting.

by Emile Berliner who invented the flat disc recording, and called his record-playing machine the gramophone.

Edison went on to patent many more inventions. When he died in 1931, a rich and famous man, the President of the United States suggested that all the people of the country honour the memory of the inventor by turning off all electrical appliances for a few seconds.

Other Inventions

Between 1880 and 1914, some of the inventions which helped mankind included the cable car, underground railways, improved refrigeration, synthetic dyes, electrified railways, magnetic recordings, alloy steel, improved artificial fertilisers, artificial leather, and the gyroscope.

Other inventors were working on devices equally useful if less glamorous. The first flush toilet was invented by Thomas Crapper. A great impetus was given to business by the introduction of the typewriter. John Cross invented an improved expanding fireman's ladder. George Eastman perfected new film both for ordinary photography and for cinema work.

It must be remembered that throughout history there were unsuccessful inventors, as well as successful ones. This is as true of the Victorian era in Great Britain as of any other time. Men spent a great deal of time and trouble in working on inventions which either failed to work, or were of little use when completed.

One example of this was a device of Henry Bessemer, inventor of the steel-making process. He also tried to invent a cabin which would remain stationary no matter how much a ship rolled in heavy seas. Before the first trial voyage, Bessemer issued a statement which declared:

> Mr. Bessemer's hydraulic apparatus is an established certainty, and not a matter of speculation, and it will always insure the floor being kept level.

Brave words, but unfortunately they proved to be less than accurate. The trial was not a success, and a contemporary account observed diplomatically: '. . . the device unfortunately proved not entirely satisfactory.'

Further Reading

Pyke, *The Science Century* (Murray)
Derry and Williams, *A Short History of Technology* (O.U.P.)
Aldis, *The Printed Book* (Cambridge)
Gibbs-Smith, *A History of Flying* (Batsford)
Gelatt, *The Fabulous Phonograph* (Cassell)
Rickards, *New Inventions* (Evelyn)

8   The Great Leap Forward

Weapons of War

The 20th century saw a rapid advance in all areas of science and technology. Many of the new inventions were used for the benefit and improvement of men's lives. In 1914, however, the First World War broke out. Inventions were adapted for the purpose of taking lives, not saving them. All the brilliance and ingenuity of men which formerly had gone into inventing machines for peaceful ends were now devoted to the development of weapons of war. War on an international scale acted as a stimulus to invention—but a dreadful form of invention.

Two major developments assisted inventors to manufacture more deadly weapons—steel-making and the explosives industry. In 1841, an American called Daniel Treadwell perfected a device for fitting steelhoops round the iron barrels of guns. This invention, first worked upon by a Frenchman called Thiery, made it possible for guns to fire farther without splitting the casing of the barrels. Thirty years later, another improvement led to guns being loaded via the breach-end rather than through the muzzle.

With these strong, reinforced guns available, inventors looked for ways of propelling missiles through them more powerfully. After a number of men had experimented with the compound popularly known as guncotton, Sir Frederick Abel finally made it safe for the gunners to use. In 1867 Alfred Nobel invented dynamite.

Other inventors who were responsible for new weapons or processes which improved them, included the English army officer Henry Shrapnell, who invented a new form of shell, and Alexander Forsyth whose percussion powder made guns

47   Machine-gunners protected with masks from gas attacks. The development of such guns as the Vickers or Gatling, and the use of gas, added greatly to the horror of war and striking power of the combatants. These gas masks were of grey flannel soaked in a protective solution with talc eyepieces, and were very uncomfortable to wear.

48 This armour-plated Dreadnought battleship, pictured in 1907, was then the pride of the British navy. Notice the paddle-wheeled vessel alongside.

easier to fire. Bullets became smaller as they had to be stored in the magazines of the new multiple-loading rifles like the Lee-Enfield.

More powerful guns were invented by R. J. Gatling who developed the forerunner of the machine gun and the heavier weapon invented by Hiram Maxim in 1884. Samuel Colt invented the revolver, and in 1864 another deadly weapon, the torpedo, was invented by a Scot, Robert Whitehead.

Weapons of war were developed at sea as well as on land, as may be seen by Whitehead's invention of the torpedo. Warships were built in ever-increasing numbers, especially by the British and German navies. These ships were powered by steam, carried heavy guns and were armour-plated. Since the days of Robert Fulton men had been experimenting with ships that would operate under the sea, and by 1914 both the German and British navies possessed submarines.

Aircraft, too, were adapted for war purposes. At the beginning of the war light aircraft were used mainly for reconaissance purposes, flying over the enemy lines and reporting on troop movements, but later these aircraft were equipped with machine guns and fought aerial duels with one another, and some were designed to carry bombs. These primitive biplanes and triplanes often bore the name of their maker—Sopwith, de Havilland, Fokker, etc.

At first people thought that the war, between England and France on the one

49 As early as 1492 Leonardo da Vinci had written, 'I am building secure and covered chariots which are invulnerable . . .'. But the first tanks were not used until the First World War and the tank in this picture is one of the earliest Mark I's. Despite the fact that they tended to break down, a large number of tanks were being thrown into action by 1918.

side and Germany on the other, would be a short one. But when after the first few months the conflict appeared to have settled down to long, drawn-out trench warfare, it became apparent that the end was not likely to come quickly. In all the countries concerned, laboratories worked to devise improved weapons, while factories laboured to supply more arms and ammunition. Many refinements and improvements were made to the deadly capacity of mines, grenades, shells and guns. Some of these instruments of war were named after their inventors— the Smith and Wesson revolver, the Lewis gun, the Mills grenade, and so on.

All the same, although brought up to date and technically improved, most of the weapons used in the 1914–1918 war had been in existence for some time. Two new forms of warfare were introduced, however. These were poison gas and tanks.

The gas, known as mustard gas, was launched from containers in one set of trenches to the other across No-Man's Land. It came in yellow clouds, blistering and burning anyone with whom it came into contact. Gas masks were devised to protect troops but thousands were killed or incapacitated, some permanently, by the fumes.

Tanks were adapted from the idea intended for tractors of an American inventor called Holt. These tractors moved on long caterpillar tracks over rough country, and were much more effective than orthodox wheeled vehicles. The idea was adapted for military use by an army officer, E. D. Swinton, backed by Winston Churchill who was then First Lord of the Admiralty. Two other Englishmen, W. G. Wilson and Sir William Tritton, designed the first tank.

These ungainly-looking vehicles were put into action in 1916. They were quite successful, but many broke down and the crews found them difficult to steer over rough ground; tanks were not used as much as some people thought they should have been for the remainder of the war.

In 1917 the United States of America joined the war on the side of the Allies, bringing fresh troops and new supplies of weapons and ammunition. The war ended with the capitulation of Germany in 1918.

Inventions Between the Wars

In the period between the ending of the First World War in 1918 and the outbreak of the Second World War in 1939, many men of genius continued to experiment with new inventions. There was, however, one change of emphasis. Instead of most inventors working on their own, an increasing number were employed by industries and large commercial firms. These organisations hoped that any ensuing inventions and discoveries would help in the manufacture and marketing of the goods they produced. While a number of inventors preferred to work in solitude, others went to work for the companies which could provide them with money and research facilities.

Transport

Aircraft had been used by both sides during the First World War, and a considerable amount of research had been carried out into the problems of powered flight. With the coming of peace, a number of aeroplane designers formed commercial companies to build aircraft and use them for transporting passengers and goods.

These inventors came from all countries. There were Dutchmen like Fokker, Germans like Junkers, Englishmen like Holt Thomas, and many others. In 1924, Junkers built the first three-engined aeroplane, the G23. This was followed by two British three-engined aircraft, the Argosy and the Hercules.

In the United States of America, Lockheed designed the Vega aircraft. This machine had a metal body and wooden wings, was extremely strong and capable of carrying passengers. The first real commercial use of aircraft in the USA had been in the carrying of mail. A number of pioneers had crashed and died in bad weather, but others had persevered.

All through the period between the wars, designers worked to improve the range and passenger-carrying capacity of aeroplanes. Commercial airlines began to increase in number. In the 1920s air-cooled engines were introduced. Another great step forward came with the maiden flight of the Boeing 247 in 1933. This was followed in the same year by the first flight of the DC-1. A great feature of both aircraft was that their fuselage was sound-proofed, thanks to pioneer work done by S. J. Zand.

Experiments were also conducted with airships—powered balloons. Both the Montgolfier brothers and Santos Dumont had invented balloons and flown them, but the real inventor of the airship was a German, Count von Zeppelin, who was born in 1838. He was a man with a great liking for adventure, and he fought in the American Civil War, for the Austrians against the Prussians, and for Prussia against France. While in America he had taken a ride in a balloon, and when he was a middle-aged man he set out to design one himself.

In 1900, Zeppelin's airship made its first flight. Its design, while incorporating the ideas of earlier inventors, surprised the onlookers. The airship, or dirigible, consisted of two large gas-filled balloons contained within a framework of light-weight metal girders. It was 400 feet long and powered by two gasoline engines.

The first of Zeppelin's dirigibles crashed during its maiden flight, but its inventor was sufficiently encouraged to carry on with his experiments. In spite of setbacks and further crashes, Zeppelins, named after their inventor, continued to be improved. They were used during the war, and even dropped bombs on London; after the death of Zeppelin in 1917 other designers continued to build airships.

For a time it seemed as if airships would rival aeroplanes as a means of air

50 The great airship R101, seen here moored in Bedfordshire in 1931, crashed in France on an experimental flight to India. It was completely destroyed by fire, and of the fifty-four people on board forty-eight were killed. This disaster made the British government close down its airship research station.

travel, but a number of dreadful crashes put an end to the large-scale development of the dirigibles. The gas which filled the balloons was, unfortunately, liable to explode should it come into contact with a flame, thus making the dirigibles extremely dangerous in the event of an accident. The British R101 crashed into a hill killing all but six of the many people on board, and in 1937 the German *Hindenburg* caught fire in the USA, killing 35 of the 97 on board.

Another form of air travel developed in the 20th century was the helicopter. An earlier form called the autogyro had proved useful in landing in enclosed areas, and the helicopter was to be used in the Second World War, but achieved real prominence after 1945.

Most inventors of aircraft, however, continued to try and perfect orthodox aeroplanes. The large aircraft firms like Lockheed, Douglas, Boeing, de Havilland, Lufthansa and others provided a great deal of money for research. For a while it looked as if seaplanes capable of landing on water might be the aircraft of the future, but eventually there turned out to be too many drawbacks to their commercial use in a big way.

Throughout the period between the wars inventors continued to produce apparatus and modifications to improve ordinary powered flight. During this period there came such inventions as improved flying instruments, variable-pitch propellers, all-metal structures, retractable undercarriages, wing-flaps, and many other improvements. By 1939 passenger-carrying aircraft were flying across the world. Such aircraft as the DC–3 were capable of flying long distances at a high speed with a considerable degree of comfort. The time was to come when the development of the turbine engine was to herald the introduction of jet-powered aeroplanes, but at the outbreak of the Second World War, piston-engined aircraft seemed capable of providing all that passengers and aircrews required.

More people were travelling longer distances in the 20th century than ever before. On land, motor cars and railway trains made transport easy and relatively cheap. Men like Lord Nuffield founded large motor engineering works in Great

51 The 'Coronation Scot', the famous stream-lined steam-train which came into service with the London, Midland and Scottish line in 1937. Such coal-fired trains, elegant and comfortable though they were, were eventually superseded by the Diesel engine, and railway lines were electrified.

Britain. With different manufacturers competing with one another in an effort to sell their cars, each company had to work hard at improving and modernising their products. Thus each year saw models coming off assembly lines more and more streamlined, and the prices of cars decreasing.

Railways, too, were well patronised. The new Underground Railway in London made travel in the capital much more convenient, while the electrification of many railway lines led to faster and more efficient travel, although it was not until late in the 1930s that most suburban lines were electrified.

The train service received a great deal of competition from buses. Coach firms, too, offered long-distance travel at a price cheaper than that charged by the different railway companies. In the cities, trams and trolley buses were slowly being replaced by petrol-engined buses.

In all forms of transport small groups of men and women risked their lives testing various pieces of apparatus and endeavouring to set new world records. Sir Henry Segrave set a world land speed record in his 1,000 horse-power car *Golden Arrow,* and lost his life setting a water-speed record. Malcolm Campbell, another speed enthusiast, was also to lose his life in a speed boat crash, as did his son Donald after the Second World War.

Pilots like Lindbergh, Alcock and Brown, Amy Johnson and Jim Mollison also tested aeroplanes by flying them to their limit for long and dangerous distances. Alcock and Brown flew across the Atlantic in 1919, and Lindbergh became the first man to complete the crossing by aeroplane on his own.

It was between the wars that cycling came into its own as a national pastime. All over the English countryside, cycling clubs could be seen taking advantage of this cheap and healthy means of travel.

Industry

The period between the wars was not a good one for trade and industry. In the 1920s and 1930s there were long stretches of mass unemployment and industrial disputes. By 1922 there were well over a million unemployed in Great Britain. In 1926 the coal miners went on strike and the Government declared a state of emergency. This was followed by a general strike and much bitterness and unhappiness. Eventually the strike ended, but it left many unpleasant memories.

Ironically enough, amid all the poverty and unemployment, material standards were rising, thanks in a large degree to the inventions being developed and put into practice by the large industrial concerns.

There were many new developments in the world of entertainment. In 1927 talking pictures were produced by the American film industry, revolutionising this form of entertainment. A number of individuals were responsible for the change from silent films to 'talkies', among them the American Lee De Forest who invented both the audion amplifier and the phonofilm. The latter process developed a method of adding sound to the film strip, synchronising the words to the action.

The Bell Telephone Laboratories also produced a method of making talking films, as did the Germans with their Tri-Ergon patents. After a number of experiments with newsreels and shorter films, a singing actor called Al Jolson actually spoke a few words before launching into a song in the film *The Jazz Singer*.

These 'talkies' revolutionised the cinema industry. Patrons refused to be fobbed off with silent films, although some of these had achieved a very high standard, and insisted on their local 'picture palaces' or 'movie houses' being equipped with the new talking machinery.

Similar developments were made in broadcasting. Both in the USA and in Great Britain great interest was taken in the possibility of forming broadcasting organisations. In the USA a number of commercial stations were opened, while in Great Britain the British Broadcasting Company, later to be renamed the British Broadcasting Corporation, was opened with Mr John (later Lord) Reith as its General Manager.

The initial broadcasting equipment was rather crude, as were the receiving 'cat's whisker' sets but broadcasting became so popular that improved equipment was soon designed, and the various radio manufacturing companies devised better radio sets.

By the 1930s most households in Great Britain possessed radio sets, and many millions of people were listening regularly to the programmes coming from Broadcasting House. While this was going on, an inventor was experimenting with another aspect of broadcasting, one which was to become known as television.

The inventor was John Logie Baird. Before turning to the problems of television he had experimented with a number of other inventions, including a razor made of glass, and shoes with pneumatic soles. In order to try out the latter, Baird once went out for a walk wearing a pair of boots containing two inflated balloons. Unfortunately one of the balloons burst with a loud bang, to the inventor's embarrassment.

Baird, who was born in Scotland in 1888, was trained as an engineer and got the idea of sending pictures by radio while he was living in Hastings. He conducted his initial experiments in one room, with equipment consisting of a tea-chest, a hat box and some knitting needles. After a great deal of work he was convinced that he was on the right track, and put an advertisement in *The Times* newspaper asking for assistance in making models for his experiments.

Baird's advertisement attracted a certain amount of attention and a number of businessmen provided him with money to carry on with his work. The money did not last long, however, and after being turned down by the Marconi Company Baird received aid from the BBC.

Working in his laboratory, Baird succeeded in televising pictures of his assistant over a short distance; but he was always hindered by lack of money. A further complication ensued when he discovered that other inventors were working on different television systems, ones involving screens with a different number of lines to the one being perfected by Baird.

Eventually Baird completed his invention. On August 22, 1932, the BBC broadcast its first official television programme. Baird's triumph was short-lived. The Marconi Company had also been working on its own television experiments, and they came up with a system which was more efficient than the one devised by Baird. The BBC adopted the Marconi method and Baird was very disappointed. He went on working, experimenting among other things with colour television. He died in 1946 at the age of 58. In the year of his death the BBC restarted their television service after the war—a service which owed much to the early efforts of John Logie Baird.

52 John Logie Baird and his television apparatus in 1925. A year later he demonstrated the set before members of the Royal Institution. For some time Baird was a lone pioneer in the field of television, but he later worked in conjunction with the BBC, and regular television transmissions were begun in 1932.

There were many other industrial developments in the 1920s and 1930s. Among the inventions and discoveries turned out by the research laboratories of large concerns were transistors, fluorescent lighting, nylon, terylene and the transistor.

This does not mean that individual inventors stopped working. There are many cases of individual inventors doing all the preliminary work on an invention, even if some of them had to hand over their work to large organisations in order for them to be improved or modified. Among such inventors were Ladislao Biro and his ball-point pen; Fred Waller and the Cinerama process of motion-picture photography; Juan de la Cierva and the autogyro, and Chester Carlson and the photographic process he called xerography.

Among commercial processes which helped in the everyday life of men and women in the 20th century were increasing use of aluminium kitchen utensils, heat-resistant glass dishes, and stainless steel. New ways of tinning food helped the housewife considerably. It was during this period that plastics began to be developed. Detergents did not really come into their own until after the Second World War, but soap powders were in general use long before then.

Although hardly coming under the heading of inventions, biological research into pesticides was of considerable assistance to farmers, and helped in the production of better crops.

Advances were also being made in medical and hospital equipment. For instance, efficient pieces of apparatus for testing blood-pressure, administering anaesthetics, measuring the electrical activity of the brain, were devised to help doctors and surgeons. New drugs like the one termed M&B 693 helped to kill harmful bacteria, and in the 1940s Sir Alexander Fleming discovered the antibiotic called penicillin.

Inventors were also conducting research in other fields—those of the jet engine, atomic science and something called radar, but these were to come into their own with the outbreak of the Second World War.

Further Reading

Jewkes, Sawers and Stillerman, *The Sources of Invention* (Macmillan)
Brooks, *The Modern Airliner* (Putnam)
Gregory, *Chemicals and People* (Mills and Boon)
Lindsay and Washington, *A Portrait of Britain Between the Exhibitions, 1851–1951* (O.U.P.)
Rowland, *The Television Man, the story of John L. Baird* (Lutterworth)
de Kruif, *Microbe Hunters* (Cape)

9   Modern Times

The Second World War

It soon became apparent that the methods used in the First World War would be of little use in the second global conflict. Horse-drawn artillery units were swept aside by tanks and armoured cars. Trenches and other fortifications were passed and surrounded by highly mobile mechanized troops. Soldiers were dropped by parachute miles behind the front lines. In a short time France and Belgium had surrendered and the Germans had driven the last of the British troops off the mainland of Europe.

As the war settled down to a bitterly contested and long drawn-out affair, scientists and engineers on both sides began to develop fresh fighting equipment. The German Air Force, the *Luftwaffe,* was well prepared and attacked with hordes of Messerschmitts and other specially developed military aircraft. They were met and eventually driven off by the British designed Spitfires and Hurricanes, which won the Battle of Britain over the fields of Southern England.

Towards the end of the war, the Germans attacked Great Britain with jet-propelled flying bombs, the V-1, and then with the V-2 rockets, and over six thousand people were killed. The effect came too late in the war to affect the

53 V2 rockets like this one were hurled at England by the Germans at the end of the Second World War. Fortunately they were developed too late in the war to be effective on a large scale, but those that did cross the Channel caused considerable damage.

54   This Gloster plane of 1945 vintage was one of the early jet-propelled aircraft. The principles of jet propulsion had been known for a long time; in 1787, for instance, a ship was successfully propelled by a water-pump driving a steam engine. But the real development in jet propulsion had to wait until Frank Whittle applied for a patent in 1931 for his jet engine.

situation greatly, but the principles behind the V-2 rocket were later adapted for space exploration.

It was also towards the end of the war that the first jet-propelled aeroplanes were used. The engines for these had been developed as early as 1937 by a brilliant young RAF officer, Frank Whittle, who was later knighted. Comparatively little use was made of jet-engined aircraft during the Second World War, but they revolutionised the aircraft industry in the years immediately following the war.

At sea, emphasis was put on the construction of larger aircraft carriers. By the outbreak of the war most vessels were powered by fuel-oil instead of the old coal firing, as this was more efficient and economical. Submarines, too, played a vital part in naval strategy on both sides. The German U-boats in particular were extremely effective, sinking many Allied vessels.

Other inventions which came about as a result of the war included the Mulberry harbour, the famous floating harbour which was moved across the English Channel in sections immediately after D-Day in 1944 and quickly assembled to provide shelter for shipping taking part in the invasion of France.

There was also radar. This was the system of tracking and indicating movements by radio waves. It was used to detect the approach of enemy aircraft and installed in ships as an anti-submarine device. Radar was invented and named by Robert Watson-Watt, a descendant of James Watt, the inventor of the steam engine.

Various automatic rifles and flame-throwers were developed, as well as larger

55 *Above* Perhaps man's deadliest invention – the first ever nuclear bomb to be detonated. This was the type of bomb dropped on Hiroshima in 1945.

56 *Left* The atomic bomb explosion over Nagasaki in Japan, 9 August 1945. American, British and German scientists continually worked on the possibility of an atomic bomb during the Second World War, and the first bomb was exploded at a trial in America in July 1945. The bomb dropped on Hiroshima (and the second one, three days later, on Nagasaki) killed, maimed and injured thousands of people.

guns, but the most deadly and horrible of all weapons of war was undoubtedly the atomic bomb.

For years men had been experimenting in an effort to release the enormous amount of energy which would become available should the atom ever be split. The atom was the name given to the smallest possible particle of matter. In Great Britain men like Lord Rutherford, a New Zealander, and John Cockcroft worked on this problem. Finally, in 1932, Cockcroft and E. T. S. Walton succeeded in splitting the atom.

The possibilities of their discovery seemed limitless. The power obtained from splitting the atom could be used to run factories and power vehicles. But in the 1930s war was approaching. Scientists from many countries examined the question of whether this enormous power could be harnessed to the manufacture of an atomic bomb. Work was carried out on both sides of the Atlantic, and finally the bomb was built.

Two atomic bombs were dropped. The Germans had already surrendered, so the Japanese were selected as the victims. On August 6th, 1945 an American aeroplane dropped an atomic bomb on the city of Hiroshima, and on August 9th another bomb was dropped, this time on the city of Nagasaki; both cities were destroyed. On September 2nd, the Japanese formally surrendered.

Some of the scientists and engineers involved in the invention and manufacture of the atomic bomb were horrified at the destruction caused when it was dropped on Japan. Others argued that using the bombs had been justified because the war had been brought to an end and the deaths of many soldiers, sailors and airmen averted.

The Post-War Years

Technological progress continued after the ending of the war in 1945. In the field of medicine, such pieces of apparatus as kidney machines and artificial lungs helped to save or prolong the lives of thousands. Artificial limbs had long been

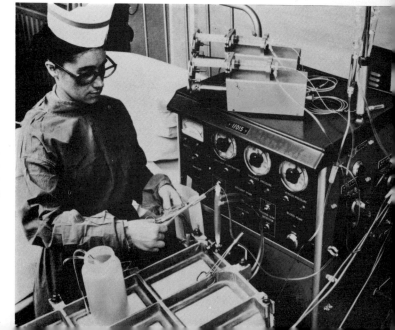

57 Kidney machines of the type seen here have saved many lives. But they are so expensive and need such skilled operation that many patients who would benefit from this treatment are unable to receive it.

58 Computers can be used for many purposes. This one is used by the Scottish station of the National Institute of Agricultural Engineering for controlling and evaluating the operation of experimental farm machinery. It has been specially mounted to withstand shocks when moved over the ground.

available, but between 1945 and 1970, a great deal of research was carried out into chances of transplanting organs from one body to another. A great breakthrough occurred when Dr Christian Barnard carried out the first heart transplant operation in South Africa.

New pieces of scientific apparatus seemed to be developing everywhere. In offices computers began to do the work of clerks. If the correct information was fed into the computers they could arrive at decisions and work out complicated problems in a short time. Today computers can be used to run machinery, regulate traffic and a host of other activities. A computer is an intricate machine into which information can be fed. From the information which is put into it, the machine is capable of making huge calculations and working out complicated problems. These machines can store information and can thus be said to 're-member' things for as long as the people using the machine want them stored. It was an Englishman, Charles Babbage, who first worked on this invention with any success as long ago as 1832.

Technology also entered education on a large scale. Radio and television sets

59 This is one of the world's largest hover-craft. A British invention, it is one of the outstanding developments in land–sea travel since the Second World War. The craft travels smoothly and rapidly over the water on a cushion of air.

were increasingly used as teaching aids, as were tape recorders and record players, especially with the introduction of the long-playing record. A method of recording and playing back television programmes meant that such programmes could be stored and used at any time.

Atomic power was used to run factories. The first nuclear-powered submarine, the American *Nautilus,* was launched in 1954, and over the next decade many others were built and sent to sea. The first merchant vessel to have nuclear-powered engines was another American ship, the *Savannah.*

Another invention, this time British, was the hovercraft. This most unusual vessel was designed by Christopher Cockerell to skim over water or land on a cushion of air. A number of complications had to be overcome, but the hovercraft attracted worldwide interest in the late 1950s.

In the entertainment industry, television became the most popular form of amusement. Sets were improved and their price reduced. The cinema fought back in an effort to keep its patrons by inventing such devices as Cinemascope, Cinerama, and many others. There was even a system by which scent was released in a cinema in order to match the mood of whatever was happening on the screen. Neither this system—dubbed 'Smellies'—nor any of the others could prevent attendances at cinemas dropping drastically.

Radio, too, became less popular, although technical improvements like Very High Frequency made listening easier. The invention of the long-playing record gave great impetus to the gramophone industry.

In industry many new ideas were put into practice. Detergents, synthetics (man-made materials), plastics, electronics, oil refining, were all developed and improved in the years after the Second World War.

More and more cars were seen on the roads of the world, and each year brought its new models. The jet-engine took over the aeroplane industry, and long-distance passenger travel became an important factor in the air transport industry. In Great Britain such aircraft as the giant Brabazon airliner and the de Havilland Comet were the pioneers in air travel, while the turbo-jet Vickers Viscount

60 The famous Concorde 001. This revolutionary type of aircraft, with its attendant noise problems, has caused great interest and created much controversy over the last few years.

attracted a great deal of international interest. These were followed by huge jet-powered planes like the Boeing 707 and the Vickers VC-10, capable of speeds of almost 600 mph, and then by the largest of all, the almost incredible Jumbo Jet.

Another magnificent achievement was the Concorde aircraft. This began as a joint British and French venture in aircraft construction and resulted in a large passenger aircraft capable of carrying 132 passengers at a speed of Mach 2.2 (approximately 1500 mph), a supersonic speed which meant that the Atlantic can be crossed in a little over 3 hours. The Concorde is capable of cruising at an altitude of 65,000 feet with a maximum range of over 4,000 miles.

Space Travel

Although the war ended in 1945, most of the major nations in the world continued to experiment with the design of new weapons and methods of transport. This was due to the mistrust felt between such countries as the USA and the USSR. Both nations obtained the help of German scientists who had been working on rocket travel when the war ended, and encouraged them to carry on with their researches. Soon both Russia and America were competing to be the first to put a man into space.

Russia gained the first advantage when, in 1957, she sent an artificial satellite, Sputnik 1, into space. It weighed 184 lbs and travelled round the earth in 96·2 minutes. A month later, the Russians launched a larger satellite, Sputnik 2, carrying a female dog, Laika, a number of instruments and a radio. It remained in orbit for five months.

The Americans realised that they were behind in the 'space-race' as it was called, and their engineers and scientists redoubled their efforts to construct and launch their own artificial satellite. Eventually, in 1958, they managed to launch Explorer I into space. In the same year they also dispatched Vanguard I. Both Explorer and Vanguard were much smaller than the Russian satellites, but the equipment they contained seemed more sophisticated and sent back clearer messages.

Many millions of pounds were spent in constructing such satellites, and the race between Russia and the USA intensified. The Russians were successful with their three Luniks. Lunik 1 went close to the moon, Lunik 2 actually hit the moon's surface, while Lunik 3 sent back pictures of the moon's surface. All three spacecraft were unmanned.

61 An historic photograph! Man walks on the moon for the first time. The American astronaut, Edwin Aldrin, makes his moon walk and conducts scientific experiments. For hundreds of years man has dreamed of exploring the heavens and now the first stage in the journey has been accomplished.

In 1961, the Russians launched the first man into space. He was a 27-year-old Russian Air Force officer called Yuri Alexeyevich Gagarin. Major Gagarin made his famous journey in a spacecraft called Vostok 1. It weighed over 10,000 pounds. A second flight was made later in the same year by another Russian, Gherman Titov, in Vostok 2.

After a number of experiments and test flights, the first American to go into orbit round the earth was John Glenn in a Mercury capsule, who made his voyage in 1962. He was followed by other astronauts—Scott Carpenter, Walter Schirra and Gordon Cooper. The Russians continued to send up their own spacecraft, including at least one flown by a woman.

It was in 1969, however, that the greatest of all space journeys were made. In that year the USA twice landed men on the moon. The first spacecraft to accomplish this was Apollo II. While Michael Collins controlled the main spacecraft in lunar orbit, two men, Neil Armstrong and Edwin Aldrin, went down to set foot on the moon. Millions of people on earth saw them do so, thanks to a television camera which the astronauts took with them. They also planted other pieces of equipment on the moon's surface, including a seismograph to send back any movements charted along the rocks of the moon.

It was Armstrong who, as he descended on to the surface of the moon made his historic remark, 'One small step for man, but a giant stride for mankind.'

Later in the same year, three more Americans made another expedition to the moon, this time in Apollo 12. While Richard Gordon kept the spacecraft in orbit round the moon, Charles Conrad and Alan Bean went on in the lunar module, Surveyor 3. They spent $31\frac{1}{2}$ hours on the moon before returning to Apollo 12 and thence to the earth.

Even these fantastic journeys did not exhaust man's ambition or ingenuity. As soon as the moon shots had been completed successfully, men set out to plan even greater things—to invent ways of sending men on past the moon to the planets beyond.

Further Reading

Savage, *A State of War* (Blond Educational)
The New Space Encyclopaedia (Artemis)
Booker, Frewer, Pardoe, *Project Apollo* (Chatto and Windus)
Bono and Gatland, *Frontiers of Space* (Blandford)

10 The Future

In the 19th century, an author called Jules Verne wrote books of adventure in which he described machines that could take men to the bottom of the sea or burrowing through to the centre of the earth. People scoffed at what they thought to be the wild imagination of the writer. Yet many of the inventions described by Verne became a fact within a hundred years.

Another writer, H. G. Wells, wrote stories of imaginary journeys into space. Again people thought that such ideas were absurd, but many of the inventions and appliances imagined by Wells were later put into practice.

Today, writers of science fiction make up stories containing inventions which seem incredible. However, so much progress has been made over the last hundred years that people hesitate to dismiss even the wildest ideas as being impossible, just in case they are one day translated into fact.

62 The first vertical or short take-off and landing fighter plane to enter operational service. It is the Hawker Siddeley V/Stol Harrier Fighter. It can carry over 5,000 lbs of cargo, and travel for 2,000 nautical miles without refuelling. At low level it can fly at a speed of about 600 knots. It has four swivelling nozzles which can direct the thrust of the engine downwards for hovering or to the rear for conventional flight.

63 A hovertrain, a form of travel still in the experimental stage. A special rail track has to be laid, and of all the forms of propulsion experimented with, the linear motor has been the most successful. The vehicle is expected to attain speeds of 250 miles per hour.

Forecasting the future with any degree of accuracy is a very difficult task, but it may be possible to get some idea of the inventions which will be devised over the next hundred years by looking at the research which is taking place today.

There will be many improvements in transport, this seems obvious. In space travel, men will seek to develop bigger and more powerful spacecraft which can take them to Venus and the other planets.

Jet-powered aircraft will become even larger. Experiments are also being conducted into nuclear-powered airships. Helicopters have proved their worth and will be improved. A great deal of further research is also going into vertical take-off aircraft. Methods of controlling the approach and take-off of aeroplanes at airports will be increasingly mechanized.

In the USA engineers are working to improve vehicles driven by electricity. Such battery-powered cars will be quieter and cleaner than petrol-driven vehicles.

In order to control traffic on the road, efforts are being made to build automatic traffic control systems. There have even been prototype models of cars steered automatically, controlled by computers. Such vehicles, it is argued, should be free from human error and thus be free from accidents.

Railways, too, will have to be modernised. It is possible that increasingly they will go underground, as they are in London, Paris, New York and other large cities. Other planners are working on monorail systems—overhead railways.

More and more machines will be taking over the work at present being done by men and women. Computers will store information and work out problems. Business men will talk to each other over telephones linked to a television set, so that they can see each other as they talk.

Spare-part surgery will become even more important. Artificial hearts and other organs suitable for inserting into the bodies of patients will be developed.

These are just a few of the inventions which will affect our lives in the future. There will be many others that are impossible to forecast. The progress of science and technology is so rapid that it is difficult to know what tomorrow will bring, because sometimes it seems that tomorrow is already here.

Index

The numbers in **bold** type indicate the
figure-numbers of the illustrations.